Favours of the Muse

Favours of the Muse

Renaissance sonnets for a modern age,
and a warning for all poets.

Henri Amlani

Ross-Evans

Favours of the Muse

ISBN 1 874498 06 7

British Library Cataloguing in Publication Data
A CIP catalogue record for this book
is available from the British Library

Printed by
The Burlington Press
1 Station Road, Foxton,
Cambridge CB2 6SW

Published by
Ross-Evans
St. Mary's House, 47 High Street,
Trumpington, Cambridge CB2 2HZ

Cover design by Chris Springham

Contents

I

Melpomene

Melpomene, I am calling you from beyond the grave, yet you do not listen to my words though they are laced with the passion and tragedy which I fed unto you for so very long and at such a price. But why do you no longer listen to me?

I know why. It is because you have found a new love, a new victim for your thirst. No doubt I shall meet them too and they will sit at your great table here, alongside the rest of your heart's blood.

And to you out there, stranger... you who are seeking the verse from these tales – read first my own story before you lay a word for her, that tragic witch whose eyes cry so shamefully. Listen to what I shall tell you before you begin with her. I beg of you, listen.

1

...I have struck a deal with God.

And so do I commence the beginning of this tale, chapter by chapter until I have written it all for your eyes and for your thoughts, dear reader. Read well, for my message will be grave.

It is true that my father has been taken by the mermaids and that he now resides with those haunting spectres of my past. It is also true that my struggle has been great, but, at last, I think that the matter between myself and the muse has been settled and I am confident that both parties are at ease with one another.

I laugh at you muse, in your deep sea-cave.

And I suppose that I must now tell you, dear seeker of tales, the story of the ordeal from whence came this bargain. Perhaps this tale will act by way of a contract, to which all of you will be my witnesses. I hope that I shall not have to call upon you should our deal be broken by either party. Anyhow, despite my concerns, I have made the deal. God has agreed to arbitrate between myself and the muse. God has seen to it, with all of His infinite wisdom, that I and the muse shall no longer hurl worlds at one another and that we shall live out our days in peace.

I *laugh* at you muse in your deep sea-cave.

I hope that God does not know what I have done to the muse. People say that He knows all, but I am not so sure. I think that sometimes the mermaids are able to keep secrets even from Him. Well, my friends, let us hope so since I have stuffed the muse down a tiny cave in a cliff by the sea, near my home. The mermaids who reside therein are holding her for me until my wife and I have long shaken off our touch with this world.

I expect the muse is painfully angry with me. I shall visit her from time to time. I shall stand above the cliffs where we fought, on nights when there is a full moon, and I shall taunt her with stories of a meaningless and boring life, a life with no tragic verse.

O, how I look forward to taunting the muse. My taunts will be her final demise. They will break what is left of her spirit, and then she will be truly dead.

I only hope that God will not be watching me at the time; perhaps I should wear some sort of disguise, and beguile God Himself. In fact, I suppose that God must be wondering right now, where, o where on earth is the muse. Ahhh.... Keep looking Lord, you shall not find her on earth. I have stuffed her away. O, how I laugh within myself, a hidden laugh; hidden from those divine eyes.

And what of the muse? Well, my friend, stranger that you are, I shall tell you this much to begin...

Take heed, when you stand alone upon an empty cliff, above a roaring sea, with the moon casting a beckoning path of light towards the open ocean. Beware of those distant stars that carry strange demons within their light. Shun the midnight breeze as it dances and sings around your body. And, if you should look upon the deep blue, where the whiteness lashes the rocks, and see there figures diving and leaping, then know that danger is upon you.

Listen not to the whisperings in your ears and close your eyes to the ghosts around you. For the muse will be there, to capture your soul and fill your life with tragedy. Run, run I tell you, for at that moment all will be lost. The magic of old, which was born with the first tear of man, will be awakened and all will be lost for you, my poet friend.

But rest now, for what more can I say? I can warn no more. All that remains for me to do is tell the tale, as best as I can; though I shall beg the forgiveness of the experts of prose, for we poets are skilled more in the art of verse than in the telling of a tale of words, and I dare but give a few of my songs here, for fear of waking the spirit of that infernal monster, the muse. Oh yes, believe me my friend, the songs are the food upon which she feeds, that infernal parasite who thrives on tragedy and broken hearts.

That was the time when I first sensed that the muse had crept within my soul and I realised that this tingling in my chest would soon become a gnawing at my heart. O Lord, why did you desert me? Did You too feed upon the joys of the muse? Did You like to watch O Lord? No? Then where were You? I know, I know what you say next... 'I was carrying *you*'. Oh, Lord, Lord, I cried for You also, I always had sympathy for You, alone upon Your cross. I know that the muse was sitting upon Your shoulder that day, I saw her there. And how like her to bring You back from the dead to write another song, as if death itself was not tragedy enough. Of course not, it is life upon which she feeds. But no longer, no longer. *I* have shut that bitch spirit away.

And then, Lord, I wrote that song for You. How did it go, let me see now? Oh yes, that's it. Listen:

If but I could prepare these lines in dark,
Then surely they should find their perfect pitch,
And set upon the ears of men their mark,
And by their darkness minds of men bewitch.
"Where were You God, when I had sunk so low?"
I turned to see sole footprints in the sand –
Where were You Lord, for footprints sole to show,
"In times of trouble, why not together stand?"
"My son, " God spoke, "put holy faith in Me,
Since footprints sole marked when I carried you,
For by your side your Lord shall ever be,
And there remain to greet your troubles new."
"Yet why the struggle mine and Yours the due?
Forgive me Lord, 'twas I that carried You..."

Do you like my words, stranger? I think that they touched a chord with the Almighty, since He has now made the deal with me.

And the struggle itself? The final battle? I don't remember much of it, though I am sure as I recount to you the story of the muse's birth I shall recall each and every detail. I know that I spoke to the mermaids after the battle. Perhaps their words will give you a good introduction to the finale. Strange words they spoke, though they did not seem so at the time; they appeared most apt as I swirled, thrashing around in icy water. The cold hurts too, you know.

"Can you see the stars in the sky, dear poet? Do they speak to you of the justice of the world? What strange demons do they

carry forth this time? Oh our dear poet, come be with us…"

"I see no demons but yourselves, mermaids. The stars are just bright lights in a dark sky. See, there is no more than that."

"O truly your muse is ours now."… Laughter, laughter, delight… *"But the stars are incredible this evening. How sad that you have lost your verse. What now shall you deploy to win your way? Mind that the moon does not hear your plain tongue."*

"There is no justice written among the stars, they shine for all, good and evil."

"Of course they do, as we have always understood. And how we have laughed at your noble pose, standing proud beneath the heavens, with honour on your mind and a crusade in your heart. Now you have felt the weight of the world. Death has touched you and you have learnt the useless expense of honour. So many souls we have seen pass by cursing their foolish pride which bought them nought but eternal end."

"There is only life and death, what use then for poetry?"

"You have it, at last. So come with us, be with us. We have touched your soul and taken an immortal life for you. You belong here now. Come, it is easy to sink beneath the waves and the pain is but a passing thing."

"To remain with you in these freezing waters, I shall not please our tragic pride, no more. I am done with you now and owe you nothing. It is you who have taken from me. Now I shall turn and swim towards my love; see, she comes through the water to catch me. You shall not take me and you shall not touch her."

"O helpless poet. You are lost without your precious muse. Should we return her to you? Once you would have smashed your way through our ring with verse so powerful that the ocean herself would have trembled and shaken at the spirits you awoke, whilst we would have writhed in agony at your deliberations. Lost you are now. Now we have your precious muse.

"Tell us poet, is your shoulder cold now, does the chill pierce

your heart as it does mine? How I wanted you, on those bitter nights when you stood alone upon the rocks. One kiss was all I asked, but disallowed was I by that very muse who filled you with the passion that we loved."

"It is my life to live, fair mermaid queen. And I have thanked you enough with a broken lover's pain upon which you have all fed. Passion has gnawed at my soul enough. Let me go in peace."

"Of course, dear poet, dear love. And we shall keep your muse within our darkest caves, which we shall seal tight with the souls of captured sailors drowned; and around the entrance we shall post mermen strong who shall be blind to their own passion and keep a watchful guard.

"Go now and love what you can of your life, love its simplicity and its beauty and we shall not meet again, I think."

"Bless you mermaids, farewell."

The muse is gone and shut away for good. And now I have lost my tongue, as you may have gathered from the mermaids' words. I have lost the power to reason with tragedy and make fine lines out of evil happenings. I have become boring. I have made a deal with God. I have stuffed the muse in a deep sea-cave. I laugh at the muse in her deep sea-cave. Oh, how I laugh at her. I have deceived the Lord himself. And I have saved the life of my wife and myself, and my children to come. I have given myself a future. And now I must tell you how, in case on one stormy and dark night you find yourself dancing with the demons in the gales upon the cliffs; in case you come face to face with mermaids, and in case you feel your heart being torn asunder by gripping teeth that will not let go; in case, one day, the muse should get you, my friend. I must teach to you the tale, from beginning to end.

The muse speaks: 'Yes, yes my poet, I can hear you too. Speak, speak and tell of our battle, tell the tale, my worthy opponent, my father, son and mother. I cannot free myself from these chains alone and now I need you again dear, dear poet. Tell the tale and teach the words. Teach them unto the lips and pens of poets out there. And then, when they are asleep, on those dark nights about which you so lovingly sing, they shall feel the tingling in their hearts. Oh yes, Oh yes. I laugh at thee poet, poor poet with your silly god. I laugh at thee, silently.

2

I have learned to believe in ritual.

I have come to fear the consequences of standing out alone, in sin. My ritual is to absorb myself into that mass of others alongside whom I sin. As I have come more to believe in what is supernatural, so too I have emphasised my practice of ritual.

I must tell you that this is a tale of the supernatural. Whether you will take my words to heart now, later or never is no concern of mine for I have already fought my battle and I now stand anxious to avoid a further fight. Therefore I shall fear the supernatural and continue my various rituals in order to keep what-should-not-be at bay.

"Do you believe in mermaids swimming free?" It was a line I had once written, a verse for mermaids. I believe in mermaids, as I believe in spirits, and as I fear the reality that is the haunting muse. *Take heed when you find yourself on that cliff above the stormy sea... lest you also should learn of the muse.*

"Lest fate should choose this day to break death's fast." Another line I had written, in honour of death. I believe in death, but do not ask me about 'beyond death'. I first learnt of death when I was four years old. By mine own realisation, as far as I can recall. I remember sitting at a low table, a table fashioned with its origins still in mind. The knots and side branches of the tree were clearly visible in the table top. I was sure that tables did not grow on trees, yet here was evidence of such. The legs of

the table, though accurately and unnaturally positioned for balance, were the real gnarled branches, twisted and painful as they had grown from the table top. Growth can be painful, they say. This tree-table hybrid which I remember so vividly hosted the evening supper for myself, my two brothers and my sister. I was the youngest.

Our supper was my mother's favourite, egg and bacon and fried bread. Now this is the interesting part. Obviously, it being my mother's favourite meal to cook, I had been eating such rubbish since I was much younger than I tell you of now. But on this day things were different for a reason that I do not know. I suddenly realised that people grow old. Why, I do not know. But it was a quick thought and led like an avalanche to questions, difficult questions: 'how old do they grow?' Which in turn collapsed in a heap with 'then what happens?'

"Then you die." My brother answered, not intending to throw me into the awaiting panic. "Does everyone die?" I queried, unable to comprehend that I might not be exempt from death.

But there was the answer, before me. Pig and not-chicken lay on my supper plate next to a greasy piece of bread. Pig and not-chicken had died and failed to exist. O unhappy life! And for what? "Why, why?" I cried, the tears pouring down my face towards the pig and egg below me.

Comfort, comfort; the attempts of mother and guilty brother were little felt as I tried to understand that I would, one day, cease to be. That I might, one day, be breakfast for someone; that I might, one day, be a table for someone, that I might never have existed so that someone could break me around their supper plate and soak me up with greasy, fried bread... as had happened to one of my brothers. Unhappy, but lucky life. How lucky to have made it this far, I thought. My eldest brother continued the comfort and stemmed the tears, convincing me that I would be ready to die after I had lived my life, which would be long and fun. I wonder if anyone is ever ready to die?

And where was God? At that time I did not know, though I know now where He sits. I had learned of death, the stalker of all of our lives. A busy spirit. I pictured him, as my tears dried. A fiendish sprite, dark and menacing and quick through the air as he rode the clouds. A spirit that would one day visit me. But, then I would be ready for him. Oh, yes, my living brother was right, I will be ready for death when he comes. But will he be ready for me?

'My living brother' you ask? Yes, two brothers sat with me at the table, both older than me. Yet only I could see them both. One alive, the other dead. One eating, the other the egg; one born alive, the other born still... but still born, at least to my eyes.

My family had accepted that all small children have imaginary friends, and that I had been blessed, or cursed, with a vivid imagination. I had not realised until now that the egg I was eating was of the same seed as my dead brother who sat watching me, in between my living brother and my sister, distraught because I was upset with realisation. But how upset must he have been with his own lot, the runny egg that he was.

O tears, stale and salty eyes. The questions that brought more and more questions until life and death had exploded around me. But surely for me it was different. I still believe sometimes that I am different; then, because I could see my not-living brother; now, because of the muse. But I must not believe it, instead I must immerse myself in the ritual of others, as we did that evening when we ate pig and egg. The collective guilt of the animal kill was split between all who partook of the flesh. Death and guilt can be eased by ritual, I have learned of it. And so as we share our guilt by consumption of the evidence, so too I think now of God and how we eat His spirit in honour of slaughtering Him. Is it a trick of the eater or the eaten? Surely God is smarter than me and the pig more stupid? But, I must not question the ritual, the conscience-saving ritual.

From that point I was aware of death, the death on my plate, the death in the table, the death sitting opposite me, and also the death within us all. Death was then one of my demons. Winged and evil, dancing in the clouds, the head of a wolf upon his shoulders. How fearful to a young boy. That night I consulted my not-living brother alone in my room, as I had often done while he sat watching me. He cried as I had earlier cried. I do not think that he had realised that he was the egg, as I was the pig. That his turn had come as mine would later. His tears were diamonds, bright stones falling onto my carpet, glistening in the light of the moon as it peeked through my curtains. I picked up the sparkling stones and hid them in the boot of a toy car for safe-keeping. The tears of my not-brother; they were precious to me, those not-tears.

My brother cried me to sleep that night and I dreamed of life and fun; a long life with lots of fun. I did not dream of the winged wolf, dark and evil as he waited to collect his dues.

~

"Oh muse, do you hear my tale? Can you hear me in your deep sea-cave? What are you thinking now? Do you like my beginning?"

Yes I can hear you dear poet…

The voice within my mind talks to me as I tell the tale. It is the muse, speaking from her deep sea-cave.

"Oh muse, you would break the bounds of death and nature itself to come and sit upon my shoulder and keep warm my tragic heart."

Of course dear poet. I am destroyed for now, trapped within this deep sea-cave, a soul stranded alone, though not quite alone. These strange creatures which always I have loathed, they taunt me with kisses and strokes. And your father is here too, dear poet. He is weeping his tears within an old glass jar, tied at the top with a small part of a fishing net and a piece of golden rope, full of hate. I wonder who put him like that, poet? Did you put him there, full of hate?

"Oh muse, you speak of the old wars, can we not let them rest now? God will be angry if He hears us."

He will not hear me, I speak with my thoughts, undetectable to even the Almighty. Though I fear He may hear your mad conversation with yourself. Perhaps He will lock you away as you have done to me. Ha!

But fear not, dear, dear poet, for already I have decided how I will escape from here. There are many drowned corpses here, their bodies embalmed by the women creatures and their souls in tiny shells. Have you never stood upon the shore and listened to the shell, the noise it makes from within? Hold it close to your ear, you will surely hear their trapped sighs. Firstly I shall shame the strong mermen, they shall miss the taste of battle after I have put epic deeds of heroism into their minds. They shall flee to seek sanctuary from their women in the heat of war. Then, I shall seduce these pathetic mermaids with my tragic art and cast love upon their frail and fish-like forms. With corpses they shall dance about this cave, into deadened eyes they shall gaze with their love and lose their hearts to water-filled bodies. I shall listen to their tragic song as they write of their love for those whose lives they have already taken. Oh yes, dear poet. Their broken hearts and weeping consciences shall fill my soul with such delight, their crying song will be my strength. I shall rise and break these chains, you shall see. And then once more, my poet, you and I shall sit together.

"No, muse, no. We are done, I know it and I do not believe you. I do not believe the voice I hear. You are not speaking from your deep sea-cave, for I know that your body and your spirit is crushed between the rocks where it is held tightly.

"I shall not fear you muse, no longer. I shall continue the tale and put an end to the lingering memories of you. I shall share your secrets with others so that they are secrets no more. I shall tell the verse to all so that it loses all of its magic. I do not fear you any more, muse."

And so now, I shall continue the tale.

~

I am still a young child, learning the very basics of existence and non-existence. I am no more than six years of age and I am walking through a small clothing store in the village near our house. My mother is leading and I am following. I am about to have a very insightful thought.

My mother is searching, her eyes gazing and flicking from rail to rail in an intently efficient manner. She is hunting for clothes to provide for her young, for me... She seeks sports clothes in this instance. The delicate truths of nature intermingle with reality, no such adventure as hunting for the meal of the week awaits us here, no. We are keeping up with society in a different manner here, ensuring that our young go uniformed and unnoticed at school. For the time of early school years is upon us and one must be properly dressed for the various opportunities that learning may offer. The clothes racks were full of football colours, reds and blues and blacks and whites; all of them glossy, shiny shirts. I despised them. I hated football, the camaraderie of it all; it still appals me now.

I would rather have been shopping for jeans. I loved jeans. I wonder why? However, since it was not I who was really shopping, I had little choice but to follow, although my mind very much wandered off on its own journeys. And, then suddenly, there it was, this amazing thought. I stood transfixed, staring at a pair of jeans hanging on a clothes rack. They were identical to the pair that I was wearing. The same colour, the same label, the same new smell. And what of the surroundings? The shop was the same as it had been last week when my mother had bought me the pair of jeans I was now wearing, from this very hanger. I looked around. The shop, the customers, the assistant, my mother, all of them looked exactly the same as they had the previous week. Glorious life! Perhaps it would not all end in the clutches of the wolf-headed, winged beast who flew in the night shadows. What if, after we died, we came back to repeat the same life over and over again? It was almost obvious and so easy to believe for a young boy.

I thought to myself that if I were to scratch my thought, with a pencil, upon a small piece of paper and put it carefully into the back pocket of my jeans, then, after I had lived and died and come again to my little life, the next time I bought these jeans I would reach into the back pocket and find a small piece of paper in my own childish hand explaining the secret of life, over and over again. Would this message containing the secret of life be able to survive the trip of death and birth, of re-birth?

Childish thoughts are often the basis for adult philosophy? Is that true, or not? To find a message from a previous life, is that not the dream of man? Is that not the answer? Would I believe those words "*you were here before, you were here before, you were here before*", would I recognise my own hand? And what would it mean anyway?

These were confusing thoughts, and are even more so now. As a child this was easier to accept. Now it means little to me, it is a thought with no substance, but it is interesting and I have noted it for the tale. Perhaps it meant that I could beat death after all. I would die in the clutches of his wolf mouth but I would be digested in his bowels only to be re-born again, from the behind of that hungry wolf. Is this why men are evil, because we have all travelled through the belly of death?

That night my not-living brother came to my bedside. He woke me and spoke to me of the trials and difficulties, of the truths and not-truths of not-life. I ventured to explain to him my new theory. We discussed our childish philosophies and I believe that they made some sense. It certainly eased my fears of the winged wolf and I am sure that my not-brother slept more soundly in that new attitude. I decided that the next day I would start hunting for scribbled messages from our former lives. It could be that there was a former life where my not-brother was my brother, no longer still at birth. Joy! It would mean that there was chance again for a happier life in the future for him. But, was life not meant always to repeat itself, as I had first suspected? Maybe it was not a heaven but a hell I had discovered here. Heaven and hell? If these are the answers, then what are the questions? I started to consider whether or not life could be changed from its constantly repeating cycle. Was this the answer to heaven and hell? Was it about how we could change our lives, for better or for worse?

I could think of it no longer. The answers must come more easily with age, I thought. I would wait until I grew older, I decided. I would not seek the messages of life. I was sure that if they existed, my mother would have told me about them. Surely she would have found them in my pockets and given them to me. Suddenly afraid of what I would discover if I searched too hard, I resolved to sleep and think no more of this puzzle until the next day.

That night I recall that another visitor solved the problem for me. I was woken in the middle of my dream by a shuffling sound. Terrified as only a child could possibly know how to be, I hid deep under my covers. I heard the noises from inside my own room. I heard grizzled whisperings and the quiet creaking open of the wardrobe doors. Then I heard the flapping of wings and then... a terrible silence.

I slept in the cave of my bed sheets that night, my heart pounding drum-like into the springs of the bed. In the morning I mustered the courage to peek out from my shelter. The room was empty, but I knew that winged beings had come that night. They had left my window undone and the new sports clothes my mother had bought for me that day, which I had left in the shopping bag, untouched except by her, were now lying on the floor of my room, their pockets turned inside out. I knew straight away that the thought of the day before was one which must remain a thought forever and which I should never try to prove or disprove. I was not sure if the winged beings were good or evil, but I knew that they had searched my new clothes for messages of life. What they had found I do not know, probably nothing. But they were a factor I did not want in my room at night again and so I would not seek the objects of their desire, I would leave them be and hope that they return me the same compliment. The dreams of darkest night could be a very frightening experience for a small child. To make sure that they did not visit me again, I picked from upon the floor a silver feather. It was a feather from a winged being, fallen from its wings as it searched through my possessions. I took the feather and hid it inside a sock in my chest of drawers. I tied the sock up with an old shoelace in many tight knots. I even asked my brother to tie a knot as well, for extra strength.

There the sock would stay and the winged beings would know that I had their wings tied up within the sock in my drawer. I knew that they would fear this and wish no longer to bother my night-time sanctity, so long as I provoked them no further. And there my thought rested.

"Is it true, muse? Do you recall those memories?"

Silence

"You are busy muse, I understand. Though I hope you are dead now, in the deep sea-cave, I feel that you can hear me, so I expect you are busy seducing your fish men."

I have told the tale thus far. I think that the muse does not answer because she did not know me at this stage of my life. She was to arrive later, but it is important that the tale is told from beginning to end. I created for myself the character that would later summon the muse and battle with her. Together we wrote the verses that were caught by youth. We fought upon the dark cliffs and in the cold sea over rhymes of lovers' folly and childish fears. I remember the lines we wrote for the small children who cried in the dark, and hid from the winged beings as I had hidden myself that night. "Shall I sing them to you again muse, in your deep sea-cave? Come now, it is not a painful song, we are just warming up now. The real pain will come later, muse. Listen...

I'd hide beneath my bed sheets for the night,
Though soon I'd suffocate for lack of air,
Yet hiding so would heal me of my fright,
And lying low would lessen so the scare;
Though darkness lingers under covers warm,
And little shield would make this sleeping sheet,
A thousand children to this shelter swarm
When agile minds do with the darkness meet.
Though little safety does this place afford,
Within our mind a fortress strong we keep,
And monsters out must with our mind accord,
And fly away when we to covers creep.
Thus see our fears by childish tricks destroyed,
In minds alone are fear and calm deployed.

"Yes, muse, of course you remember. These words are written here in my notebook, and now within the tale itself. Do they taunt you in your prison? I know that the verses to come will drive nails through your broken heart as I sit and read them here. But come, we shall suffer together as I read these songs one more time. Now I must continue the tale."

3

The tale of my youth continues at my tender age of nine; we have just moved house. We are in the same area but my parents' business is flourishing and we can afford a large house in a more tranquil setting. The new house is old, but great. It is a dread house. It fills me with awe and my father should have known that my mother would not wish to stay in such a house for long. We survived five years though. Not bad. After that time we made our second move, closer to the sea…

My bedroom in the new house was the farthest away from my mother and father's room. It was also the smallest. The bedroom itself was rather plain, but that suited me. When I slept I liked to keep things around me simple. Too many elaborate complications of furniture and décor made foul images in the shifting moonlight. But, despite all of that, it was to be in this place that the nightmares began, and they would not end until we made our second move, closer to the sea, where a different sort of nightmare would begin…

Toys occupied huge boxes in the corner of my room. They would have to wait. I needed to concentrate on the more important artefacts of my youth. As soon as my father had finished reconstructing the drawers for my clothes, I hid the feather of the winged being deep inside, still within its sock. Contained. No winged beings would enter this room. On the top of my drawers sat the very special toy car, its small boot full of diamonds made by not-tears. The new locale soon resembled the old in respect of the bare essentials, the artefacts of my already strange existence. New cupboards held old clothes and old chests sat in new corners. We made ourselves at home in our excellent new house.

Exploration was a priority of course. The house had two very appealing places. They were the two attics. A house with twin attics! It was fantastic and terrifying at first as we cleared away the old rubbish that had been deposited by previous owners. There were two because of the strange shape of the roof. My father had constructed narrow, but pleasing wooden staircases climbing up into each after a little while of our being there, and with this easy access I was able to make these places my special haunts. They soon became full of toys. Toy soldiers, toy cars, toy spacecraft. Each period of toys interacted with the other. Tiny British commandos held out in their stronghold, constantly bombarded by Imperial space-troopers: the commandos' only hope of rescue was to make a break for the rail-track and a train to the other side of the world. But little did they know that two giant dragons often slept upon the track and devoured any trains which tried to pass them. The warm summer days were always the best for inspiration. The hot sun warmed the sturdy timbers, and ideas fed my imagination, their intensity obviously increased by the action of heat. Even romance must obey the basic laws of physics, after all. The sun brought much of the fighting to a halt. German tank crews rested underneath their vehicles and sat with Monty's Eighth Army Corps, telling each other their adventures. Many a tall tale of action was exaggerated by these plastic figures as they entertained my mind.

Oh happy days, warm in the summer sun, trapped by the greenhouse effect of the attic. Whilst writing those adventures to my mind, I think I decided that I would like to become an author. I wanted to make immortal the tales of the silver knights who built their castles in my attic. I wanted to make adult the childish fancies as they clashed in motionless battle, their still figures made alive by my mind. And I was comfortable with the thought. A writer I might become. At least that would give answer to all of those annoying aunts and uncles who pestered me with the usual cliché questions.

Indeed, my imagination thrived throughout this new house. The long summer holidays gave way to the dreams of the garden. A huge garden accompanied the house and it bordered a recreational park, where there was a river at the bottom. My brother used to fish with his friends in this river. My sister used to take long walks with boys across the park to the shops at the other end. There they would take coffee and shop until evening. How they could leave the house for so long I could not understand. My world was within the grounds of this magical place.

Often my not-brother would play with me in the attics, but he spent much of the time these days sleeping. He slept at the foot of my parents' bed, on the carpet. I knew that only I could see him. Of course I had learnt long ago not to talk of him or to point him out. It always served to my disadvantage. Sometimes I thought the cats could sense him, as they curled beside him, snuggling into the well of his legs. But, I was never sure, and over the course of the years in this house, my not-brother visited me less and less. Imagination was the answer. While my mind thrived with the adventures it held within, so too did all of the spirits of the house. Yet, I found later that evil often walks arm in arm with good, and my happy dreams soon turned to nightmares. But I must not rush ahead of myself. I must explain how my imagination created the first of my adventures, how the nightmares surfed the back of my overactive imagination and how I fought back against the wolves and vampires of my dreams to vanquish them, but in the process kill my not-brother.

The most noted of my childish pasttimes was the tale of the great dragon I named Signa. Signa was an old and wise dragon, but with a fiery temper fit to lay waste the most noble of those who passed unfortunately by him. Why this great beast was unable to tame its own temper I am not sure, possibly because I was a victim of the stories around me to a great extent and there had to be a war to fight. There must be maidens to rescue and deeds to execute, but so too there must be wisdom in the fool, a gentleman in the beast.

"*The Tales of the something or other Mountains*" was to be the adventure's vehicle. I was never happy with it, of course. I was too young to write anything serious. It was simply the satisfaction of my imagination which was achieved by the tale, as though something were already necessary to feed that terrible muse. These short scribblings in childish hand breathed life into comic, armoured dwarves and poison lizard-dogs. A small child named Peter found himself lost in this world one day as he wandered where he should have not. This child was brought to speedy adulthood as he learned the lessons of death and hate in the world of Signa the Great.

And I was happy to write the tales. My youthful mind flourished. It was during these first years in the new house that I found the true potential of my dreams. Before I slept at night I would spend an hour 'night dreaming'. Like day-dreaming, but at night-time. The difference being that I was awake and plotting my own course in the dream rather than being asleep and in the hands of the dream angels and the dream goblins. (It is true that there exist such creatures. If you do not believe me look underneath your bed after a terrible nightmare... if you dare. You will see them scurrying away.)

These night-time day dreams idolised me. I was the great warrior that all boys wished to be. My battle wounds were history upon my body. A saga developed where armies clashed, castles fell and heroes were made. When I drifted to sleep sometimes the dream would continue, and that was the true magic. The dream angels are so much better at creating the image than me.

Oh beautiful dreams. At least, until the dream goblins arrived, riding their black mares through the sleepy mist, bringing with them restless and disturbing lessons.

Sometimes I would be very lucky and slip from my body during my sleep. I would find myself floating with the cold night air in the light of the moon, clouds drifting around me. I would see the sea below me, the waves crashing on sharpened rocks. It was always a sight which terrified me and so often my spirit would flee back to its corporeal home. But, where did all the magic go wrong? Such a fruitful mind, I had at this time. But being fruitful and keen to harvest, it was, of course, too easy for a foul crop to be sown.

I can still to this day recall with vivid reality the time my living brother asked me to sit with him and watch a programme he had recorded on video late the night before. Too late it was, even for his maturing age. We sat and watched.

"You'll like this." He genuinely believed it, and I sat transfixed through it all.

"*It's not scary is it?*" I should have asked but failed to do so. I wanted to be scared. The movie heightened my imagination with its daring move across the borders of tame viewing.

"*No, No! Stay away from me ! Aaaaggghhhh….!*" The cries rang from the television set and ricocheted around my brain. The howling! The howling!

I sat sweating, gripping a pillow and hoping the daylight peeping through the curtains would comfort me. But I could not ignore those eyes. Those dread and evil eyes which hung while the background faded into credits. The howling still echoed inside. The visions of torn throats and running along darkened, wooded paths, tripping and being caught; these visions haunted me. A parasite of evil had entered my brain. My first horror movie.

"Are you okay ?" My brother asked.

"Fine. Shall we watch it again?" And I did, later on, when none were around. Oh, the spell with which it gripped me was profound. I hated horror movies. Vampires and werewolves. I had not known so much of their evil until now. And I was certain that these beasts existed. What had been that winged being in my room that night? Do vampires carry silver feathers upon their wings? I don't think that they do.

My mother noticed the change.

"Muuuuuum..." I used to cry at night from my sheeted shelter, not daring to lay a hand outside for fear of it being gnawed away from my body. Sometimes it was two hours before my terrified cries brought her to my room. So far, so far. How could you do it, mother? I, the most fragile, the furthest from your arms at the most perilous time.

My not-brother came often from his room in the attic and fought outside my door in the corridor of our house. I heard him tackling God knows what beasts on my behalf. I can never believe that the din did nothing to wake the sleeping family, other than my frightened self. The doors seemed to shake some nights. One night a crack appeared in one of the panels. I and my knightly toys took the blame, but my father did not recognise the claw marks, mistaking them for the wooden sword he had known he would regret making for me.

My dreams were haunting. I ran across the recreational park next to our house one night. A wolf was chasing me. It was not death, or the dream of death, for this wolf ran with legs and did not take to the air. I ran, knowing it was near behind. I reached the house and the open sliding windows. I ran inside and turned quickly to close the barrier. I stretched out my arm to grip the handle. Moist and warm, it entered the mouth of the wolf. My scream was paralysed, silent. I woke. There was silence and stillness, but I sensed so much more than that. I took to my shelter and sealed the sheet around me, and waited.

"Muuuuum!" And then the sniffing at the door came. Picking

noises poked at the door, trying to ease underneath. I heard the footsteps of my not-brother trotting along the corridor. A muffled howl and a fighting grunt. A bang at the door and a fall to the floor of two wrestling bodies.

"Muuuum!"

No wolf entered the room that night. The next day I found my not-brother sleeping in the attic. He was cut and still bleeding from a hideous gash across his face. His hands were covered in blood and a small necklace lay in his hand, clutched by strong fingers. He opened an eye, he knew I was there. He reached up to me and offered me the necklace.

"The spoils of your latest victory."

I took the necklace. It was a lace, with three teeth strung upon it. Teeth still covered in dried blood.

"The fight was yours brother, you should keep this."

"But the beast was yours, brother," he replied. "Mine was the easy task. You have to live with the demon."

I cried in the attic while he returned to sleep. My life had suddenly changed and my family was bothered by my constant nightmares. It is true that my mother also grew tired and weary of this immense house. A safety risk she called it, far from the neighbours and exposed to thieves. She acquired a dog, a German Shepherd. Even this great beast did not last long. It fled from the house one night. It squeezed itself through an open side-window. Far too small for it, since blood was left on the frame where she had grazed away her flesh. The others mourned this strange and unexplained disappearance. But I knew and my not-brother knew, since we had watched in the moonlight from my room as it ran along the drive-way and towards the park being chased by monkeys. Monkeys who had earlier scaled the walls and danced mad steps outside my window. I like to think that our dog made a good account of itself and perhaps even vanquished the monkeys. As she ran the monkeys grew separated, some slower than the others and it is my hope that our dog turned and beat each in turn into pulp with its powerful jaws. Yet, we never saw the dog again. I fear that the whining yelps myself and my not-brother had thought we had heard in the distance were those of our own beast as she lay helpless and bloodied under a pummeling of gnarly and knotted, hairy fists.

It could go on no longer, I decided, and I took action. Twice in my life a prayer has been answered so directly that it was without doubt a true solution from the Almighty Himself. Once on this occasion and once later when I was studying at the old university. From that night on and every night for the next few years I added a simple spell to my prayers, which I muttered again and again. I added the lines " *and please dear God, don't let me have any bad dreams or nightmares tonight*." I recited these lines over and over at least fifty times each night, until I believed that they worked.

And work they did. After about a week the nightmares eased in intensity and in frequency. After a month they had gone almost completely. But with this peaceful and easy sleep came a complete lack of any dreams at all. Nothing entered my mind from sleep until wake. So too my imagination suffered. The stories of great dragons and black knights became stale and fragmented. I wandered my old haunts looking for the beings of my mind that once were, but none answered my calls. So too my not-brother was to be found less and less. No longer did I hear him wage bloody war outside my night-time door. No more did we converse on topics we had in mind. He was hardly to be found. And then, one day, we suddenly decided to move, to a new house far away, near the sea. The move happened very quickly, and much was left behind, most notably my nightmares and my not-brother. All I took of him was his diamond tears and his wolf-teeth necklace. My prayers had killed him and I was hardly ever to see him again.

I heard of him only one more time after that occasion. I was following my mother through the streets of the city, on a shopping expedition. As we struggled through the crowds a young, but strangely dressed woman came to my mother from a shop doorway. Blankets littered what was obviously her home in that doorway. The shop was not open; it was a 'misty window' shop, as I liked to call them. I did notice a small pair of eyes staring out from underneath one of the blankets of the home from which this gypsy lady sprang. I cannot decide whether they were the eyes of a small child, curled up sleepy and frightened of the crowds, or if they were the eyes of some devious sprite. However, the words this gypsy lady singled out for my mother were disturbing to me.

"Oh Mrs, Mrs. Some money for a tale, some money for your fortune ?"

"No thank you." My mother was scared of gypsies. My grandmother had told the tale to us one night of the great family curse that had afflicted her sister and her family. A simple rebuff to a gypsy and an empty hand of change had resulted in three family deaths that year, two of them infants. I don't believe that it was true but my mother was always scared of gypsies.

"I can see you. I can see you. You have three children, you should have had four but one died."

"No thank you," my mother's words were slower and more awkward. It was the first time that I ever heard a stranger speak of my not-brother. It was the last time that I ever heard anyone speak of him. My mother must have wondered about my instant tears and silence on the way home. She must have wondered, since he was not-born years before I was born. Perhaps she understood the bond. Perhaps she also could see him.

~

"Muse, muse, do you hear my tale now to answer me, to give me your worthy opinion?"

I hear you, poet. The tale is yours still. I have not yet arrived at your story, though I am seeking you out.

"Yes, yes seek me out for you are about to enter the scene, dear muse. The conception is next. I have told of the foundation, next we will witness your birth in that place by the sea, both dreadful and beautiful."

You will do me honour with the conception, I am sure of it. It is an important chapter that you are about to tell o poetic friend, so tell it true. Tell of your friends and the summers of fun; tell of your first kiss and your first love; tell of betrayal, your love and your greatest friend; not childish coupling, for it was love eternal to be, but they did not understand, those foolish children. Yet, through the tragedy of that fateful coupling I was born, the muse, released once more. I came to being in the tear of your eye as I slid down your face, trapped for a thousand years in a spellbound vial which you had found in the sea. I grew inside your tear and nurtured on the goodness within. Free, after a thousand years. Poet, I cannot tell you what it was like, how you and I are bonded, so strong it is. I think of what it would be like if you had not found the vial that day and if I had still been trapped. Oh, but of course I am still trapped. But what fun I have had getting trapped again. And now your father sits in the same vial in which you found me and from which I was freed. Irony, irony, tell me a better tale...

Dear, dear poet, tell of the first songs that you and I wrote together. You never knew that I was there, those first years I was a secret sitting upon your shoulder cold. Poet, tell now, tell now of what it means to be like you and I. Tell the song of the poet so that your tale may be easily understood.

"Your words are painful to me muse, even now. I shall. I shall tell of the poet, the being I was becoming. I shall tell it in sonnet form, muse, as we wrote it. How did it go?

Illiterate men would read this poem best,
A blinded man might see the lines most well,
Whilst deaf the man to hear above the rest,
And dumb the soul to others these lines tell.
The poet's verse, profound unto the muse,
Is sorrow foreign for a happy soul,
These loveless poets happiness refuse,
Their evening hour prefers a tragic role.
No coupled walk across a moonlit bay,
No listening ear to hear the names of stars,
No soothing touch or soul on which to lay,
Sad company to while away the hours.
While evening bodes of lovers wrapped as one,
The poets freeze, their bodies wrapped with none.

Oh yes dear poet, what fine lines here to fit your tale. How prophetic of the tragedy here to unfold. Do continue, please, lest we lose the mood.

"I shall continue, muse. While you are yet safe inside your deep sea-cave, I shall continue the verse and bleed you until your last for I cannot fear each night that you may return to haunt me. Oh muse, if I tell the tale again I shall kill you, locked as you are in your deep sea-cave. How will you survive another thousand years?

Silence…

"I shall go on dear muse, you that are the silent voice inside my head. I shall go on…"

~

To continue, I must describe our new location. I shall not tell the tale as the muse wishes me. I will not tell of the conception, not just yet. The foundation for the conception is not yet complete.

It started by the sea... It started by the sea...

I was a young teenager when we moved to the sea. I had learnt of death, I had lost a not-brother. I was a mystic and hermit to my own kind. A young boy happy in his own company until now. But with my not-brother gone and my imagination badly damaged, I easily slipped into the world of my convention. This place by the sea was to offer me the best friends of my youth, and eventually my first love.

My father's new business was a small shop in the small town. It was busy during the summer and empty during the winter. The seasons became more relevant to us as we lived in this place. The summer would be better than ever before and the winter worse. Autumn would be much cause for sadness. It was during the summer months that I was to meet my new friends. Their names were Justice and Tiny (who were brothers), Autumn and her sister Justine, and the great and amusing Mr. Lawrence, who would have been better known as the laughing fat man. His young son was accepted with grace into our new gang and in return the father treated us like allies and young adults, a complete contrast to the actions of the parents of Justine and Autumn who were to take a very defensive stand at our later interest in their daughters.

O happy summers gone, when my friends visited from the big city to spend their few weeks holiday by the sea with me. My parents became great friends with my friends' parents. Everything seemed perfect. The summers when they came were the highlights of my unimaginative life. The first two years were full of childish fun, but the third year was different and the fourth also. Things changed with age. But I must not get ahead of myself again.

"Muse, muse are you still listening?"

Yes, yes I am here, attentive as always, learning as always. Tell of the kiss.

"No, it's not yet time for the first kiss, muse."

Not the first kiss you fool. Have you forgotten me already? The traitor's kiss, how you were betrayed by Justice itself, who abandoned Justine for your precious dying season. Oh glorious fate that brought you together.

"I am telling, muse."

We called him Justin, at his own demand. "A mistake on the bloody birth certificate."

Right!

"They wrote Justin, but it got smudged and looks like Justice apparently, I've never even seen it myself, but they say they like it and they have to call me it by law." It was a well-rehearsed speech. And he would be my best friend. His brother was Tiny, and indeed he was younger and smaller than us. He would grow up to "get all the girls"; how our parents can predict such events was beyond me at that age, but needless to say I hear that he did grow up to "get all the girls". He was a good friend too. These friends were my best. My school friends in this new place by the sea were good friends to me, but my summers were not for them.

The laughing fat man was a leader to us. He would take us all in his car to the beach. His confidence would help us into the sea on rough days, when the waves were frightening. We would jump and dive off high rocks into the raging sea. We all grew to have a certain familiarity with the places where we spent our time, the beach and the sea and the cliffs. At night we would often have barbecues on the beach. The laughing fat man would provide the food and the cooking stove. He and his wife would sit and watch us have our fun as we played rough games on the beach in the fading sun. Sometimes he would buy us a crate of cheap beer and we would sit in the gardens of the holiday homes where they stayed and drink in the summer evenings, staring up at the night-time sky. Blessed night-time sky, what secrets you hold. Now I realise the enormity of it all, but then, things were different, the night sky was the moment's pleasure. "One, two," we'd count, as shooting stars flared across the heavens. "Another," we'd signal, not realising that the simple count of a falling rock in the atmosphere to us was the unfathomable drop of a failing angel from the seat of heaven. The mermaids were to teach me this later on and curse me for the pleasure I had felt each time I saw the stars fire across the sky.

"Shall we go to the castle tonight?" One of us would always ask at some point in the evening. The castle was an old fortress on the coast which was our occasional haunt. Once there we would usually split into separate groups. I would inevitably end up laying on a battlement with Justice Justin himself and talk the talk that young men know.

"You know I'll never smoke." I commented as he offered me a cigarette one night. "But I reckon all my friends will, most of them do now anyway."

"It'll take a lot of will power."

"No. It's not that. I just don't need it, my dad smokes about fifty of these things a day. I just know that I don't want to be like that, no matter what friends say."

"Me too, there's lots of things my dad does that I don't ever want to do, so that I'm not like him. Maybe that's why I smoke, because he doesn't."

"You remember that time last year when we buried Tiny in the sand down there on the beach, where that car's headlights are shining?" I pointed at the car's signal, perhaps some lovers lighting the beach as they chose a comfortable parking place to relax for the while.

"Completely, he had the mask and snorkel on so he could breathe."

"Then he jumped up when those people walked by, scared them to death."

"And that other time when we buried old Lawrence's legs in the sand so it looked like he didn't have any, and then those people went past him and he sat with the bucket of coins in front of him…"

"That was so funny. I still can't believe they put money in it for him."

"Some good times we've had here."

"Yeah, it's good. I wonder what the girls are doing. Shall we go find them?"

"Your brother will be with them."

"We'll have to get him away from them one night, so we can sit and chat, just the four of us."

"And which one would you particularly like to chat with?" The conversation was exactly what we wanted to discuss.

"I think you should talk with Autumn and I'll have a quick word with Justine."

"Sounds interesting already."

We talked well of these things and took delight in the pleasures of our age. That year nothing happened between any of us and the fun continued as usual. The next year we were sixteen and things changed, slightly, for the better, I might add.

It happened that love was breathing her evening warmth upon us one night as we lay watching the stars. A game of hide-and-seek rather expectedly found us grouped in pairs and isolated after a short while. I found myself with Autumn, the dying season, and Justice played court to Justine, while Tiny tried cigarettes for the first time that night and was content to hide himself away for fear we'd tell his parents.

I'm sure that it was the same for Justin but for me that night was one of the most memorable of my life. The night I first kissed the pale shades of Autumn as she smiled at me in the moonlight. I recall her cold cheeks and fresh breath, so fresh. I think that perhaps the first time you kiss someone, it is always the freshness you remember. Things grow stale later on. But, tonight was special. Her breath was crisp, as leaves ready to fall, her eyes were glowing with all the subtle pastel of trees in September, and her mouth was a delightful embrace into a cave of the unknown... but it was winter which waited for me at the other end.

That summer had suddenly become very special. My conversations with Justice grew less frequent since we had new best friends now, but they were always about the girls when we did speak. We continued to have the same fun on the beach as before. We played the same games, swam in the same rough waves on stormy days, we drank and barbecued often and we never ignored the laughing fat man just because we now had girlfriends. The following summer was to be the same. I knew that my relationship with Autumn was more serious than that of Justice and Justine. From my conversations with my friend I knew that there were other girls with him during the year, in between the summer months. It was not like that with me. I was in love for the first time in my life. O love, love, great big happy love. That first night, after we had kissed, my heart raced as I slept in bed and I relived the entire experience. O happy love, it must be the best thing in life. Fresh, love.

During the periods in between the summer I used to keep myself very much to myself. My school friends knew Autumn, I had shown her off many times to them and I know this made them jealous since she had hair like the strokes of a painting and eyes like polished shells of bright colour on the beach. I missed her and during my time spent alone I felt that I could be with her.

One year I decided to invite her over in October, for a week, during the half-term holidays. Never had I looked forward to something as much as I did that holiday. I often look back at my old school books from those days and find a little home-made calendar marking how many days until she would arrive, all the days crossed off in turn, in different coloured pens. Oh happy time that was to be. Autumn in October and then again in the summer, with my other friends. Wondrous days, wondrous feelings.

And then, one night about two weeks before she was due to arrive I received a telephone call from her, which was quite usual, but the content was to be different this time. As I tell the conversation to you I shall not speak her voice or her words since I cannot still abide to hear them, evil that they were. I heard giggling over the line. I knew then I was in trouble. The tone was dead, the voice was changed, and then quiet. "What is it?", I asked. Her new boyfriend! No, it could not be. Impossible that he had taken my place and had demanded she tell me while he made her laugh over our conversation. There it came, a tearing pain, quick and sharp in my chest, then an ache, a dull and powerful ache, another tearing and shooting sensation and the ache again that would never to this day disappear. The doctors have examined me, recognising something not quite right with my body. They laughed when I told them that it is a broken heart, but it is true, when true love is broken, hearts really do break. "What about the holiday?" She still wanted to come, she had happy memories of the place and the ticket was paid for. I agreed because I thought I could salvage my true love and rescue Autumn before the clutches of winter arrived. Pathetic and hope-driven I was, as are many men at some point in their lives; like a failing religion, I followed her and wanted her back. So she was still to come, perhaps there was still time for us to be together.

But that night was to be a dark night. With my broken heart I walked outside into the night air and kept walking until I was at the beach where we would often go. I walked along the sand and headed for the sea. I stood looking out to sea, the cold waves occasionally lapping at my wet shoes. Conception is a lovely thing, yet birth is so painful I am sure. Conception was now followed by birth, and mine was the pain. In the light of the all too familiar moon I saw an object washed toward me with the next wave. It was a small object and it reflected at me slightly in the pale light. The wave brought it right to my feet and I picked it up. It was a small glass vial, nothing particularly special it seemed, but worth taking home despite my grave matter. I lifted the glass lid from the lip to see what it contained. Nothing but water poured forth when I upturned the vial.

But it did not, did it muse, I know that now. From out that unlucky vial in the light of the moon where I stood with tears crawling upon my face there slipped a spirit, a spirit of tragedy that immediately saw my bleeding heart and fed upon me as new-born feed upon the goodness from which they have just hatched. Terrible, terrible night. Thunder moaned in the distance.

Seeing and feeling nothing, I put the vial into my pocket and continued my vigil of pain. That night I wanted to die. I had learnt what pain was. But I was soon to learn what suffering was, and hate. Hate? I do not think I ever hated Autumn, though I had good reason. I do not think that one can ever hate their first true love. I returned home to bed and did not sleep for three days. School was very painful but everyday life soon brought me to the day she arrived, on that bleak October day.

I know now that the muse began her work immediately. Upon my shoulder she sat and warmed it through. I adopted a certain mystique, a glaze in my eyes if you like, which others recognised and about which they knew not to enquire. My love, my love, my only love, my true love, now in the hands of some bastard who did not love her as I did, who could not love her as I did.

How would he know the magic in her eyes, the warmth of her hair, the freshness of her kiss? She was but a play-thing to him. And she, she, how could she? Well, in fact, things were about to get worse.

My lost love arrived a short time later and greeted me with a cold embrace. She had changed, she was dead; a dead love inside an alien body. This woman before me had found a new love in life, and it was not the boyfriend she left behind. This soul that confronted me and stayed with me that week in our place by the sea was a girl who had found that being drunk was a delight with which she could play. She had suddenly learnt to use her beauty in a terrible way. I remember the night, how could I not, it is etched in my heart, when she, drunk beyond control, played kissing games with a group of my friends from school. How my heart was wrenched as I watched this evil game. What she had sacrificed for this new love back at her home she now discarded anew here. She had thrown away my love for a love she had kept in faith for less than a month. What better way to break a poet's heart? When she left I was relieved more than anything, I could have stood this pain no more. That week made me hate pubs and night-clubs. I despised the meaningless friendship with which I now associated those places. I hated the short skirts, the big, drunk eyes, the painted nails around cumbersome pint glasses, how base it all seemed. I would play no more part in this game, there must surely be reward for a man elsewhere, surely some princess who did not linger with such crowds.

I was not a laughing-stock at school, though a few comments slipped by my ears. My Autumn had been a beautiful girl and people were sorry that such beauty had been tainted by such evil, though some of them had enjoyed the pleasure of that hour. I think too that the muse inside of me kept others at bay. The muse, as it lay hidden, invisible upon my shoulder: this foul creature protected me from the childish comments and jokes of my counterparts; it wished me to play a different tune and it kept me fresh for the show.

The greatest death was to come that summer, still a time when all the old summer friends met. Autumn, whom I hoped would have travelled beyond such a winter of evil, turned one night to Justice as he sat drunk in the shadows of the rocks upon the beach. I who had been sitting upon a perch of rocks nearer the sea could see their every move. They were not aware that I saw their passionate, alcohol-filled kiss, that I witnessed the worst betrayal a friend can perform upon another, that I noted with hate the vengeance that I would one day bring upon whatever evil power had brought about this situation. I am sure that the mermaids watched me that night and saw the muse sitting in the moonlight upon my shoulder. Such a sight for the mermaids. A new poet, a new song writer who they knew then would visit this place often and cry melodies of verse into the dark waters. Could they, then, have possibly realised the terrible outcome of this scenario?

Oh tragedy, you have lived with me. "Muse, you are listening to my tale I know. Have I done you justice? I have delivered you unto the story."

You have spoken indeed of my birth, O happy birth. Tell the words, let us begin, tell the words that first we sung.

"O muse, if I tell them will you not be writhing in agony, knowing that they can never be again ?"

Of course, the agony, the tragedy, you know that it is my destiny. Tell the words.

I think that the first words were not in sonnet form. Just some play-things with no tragic discipline, though with a certain beauty of their own. I wrote them during an English lesson at school. I do not remember the subject of the lesson. "Were they not something like this muse?"

How can I rest,
When the silent patter
Of tempting feet rings through my mind?
From outside that door,
I hear the screams of passion,
Calling to my despairing mind,
Pulling at my untouched body,
Tearing my limbs apart,
In a world of emotions
That can never be quenched.
But she does not realise my pain,
She cannot realise what I suffer,
For soft innocence prevails from her body,
And thoughts for a happy tomorrow
Flutter through her ignorance.
So I lie here,
Fighting despair, fighting the pain,
Justifying her feelings
To comfort my soul.
'What emotion is it I am feeling?'
I ask myself over and over..
Am I like those others?
That hierarchy of animals
Who know only aggression,
Driving them on to another tomorrow,
How I need to be different,
To dispel those tempting sounds
She makes without my door,
How much do I deserve
To be different?
Is this what she wants?
Or must I lie back,
In pain

And let life run its course,
While I wonder what my tomorrow would have been...
How can I rest?

O muse, the lines are not good, but they were the first, when we were very young."

How happy I am to hear them again, O poet I am missing you so much now as I hear your story. I must free myself from these infernal mermaids or I shall surely perish from want.

"Yes muse, I want you to perish."

First words, indeed they are awful, I am not sure why we wrote these together, those dots and broken lines, no form, no verse, no scan. Despicable, are they not? 'I wish these lines in Sonnet form were writ.' Was that not what we wrote?

"To tell the time-past tales with finer face,"
A shameful mind declares they are not fit,
"Yes, yes go on..."
And shall not live within this story's space.
"But Cupid's head is raisèd from his sleep,
For him, disturbing passion has no form,"
Indeed it does not...
"He asks me so these lines of love to keep,
Thus new I'll write and loss I need not mourn."
Yes, always keep the verse you have created...
"I glance upon those words with lover's tears,
Deceased is light yet shadows linger still,
Betrayal's dreams are yet amongst my fears,
And cross-eyed love I still would like to kill."
But sweetest memories do stir my mind,
For first love's mark upon these lines is signed...
"Yes, muse, yes it was."

O poet, do not leave me to perish here, look at the songs we can create together for the entire universe to enjoy, do not leave me with these fish creatures.

"Muse, the world has fed enough upon my tragedy. I shall continue the tale and leave it as a lesson for future men, in the hope that he who next finds your trapped soul will not release you as did I. And now I shall carry on the tale."

From that time I would often wander at night in the places where I and Autumn used to go, in the haunts of our love where I hoped that there still lingered some magic. Sometimes I would sit for hours and stare out to sea, listening for the sounds of I am not sure what, simply listening, I suppose. Sometimes I would think of lines, verses in my mind to describe the feelings. It eased the pain. I would even scribble them down and fiddle around with the verse until I was happy. Reading back the poem I had written was comforting indeed, it almost justified the tragedy. Perhaps there is truth in the words of the muse. I am still entertained by some of our verses. They calm my thoughts even now, as I recall the words we sang together…

Sun shine on me, for pale is my soul,
And darkness claims my every waking hour,
This place where meets the sea shall make me whole,
And scenes of breathless grace will give me power.
Bright pearls upon the crested sea do flash,
Blue skies are paintings touched by hands divine,
The waves upon disfigured rocks do crash
A timeless rhapsody of notes sublime.
I feed upon the weightless thoughts of birds,
Yet always passion's curse will feed my mind,
And mercilessly turns my thoughts towards
The sin of lust, where I shall evil find.
Speak not muse, for now my soul's at war,
Your pleasant lines my feelings would abhor.

The muse was born, conceived by an evil coupling of souls, released from her prison by a lost lover to feed upon the tragedy, a creature of neither male nor female purposes, but a creature with only one drive – to play tragedy unto its own heart. And the tragedy would live until the muse was dead. My grief continued for a short time in my home, but then a fantastic opportunity came to leave home and start again. I succeeded in winning a place at a university in another part of the country, as did many of my friends. School friends would meet from hereon in the holidays, to boast and tell stories, and other than that we would all gradually drift apart and make new friends and build new lives. The things we had learnt thus far, the scars we carried, were now to be our characters which we would take and present to our new friends in our new lives. My time was to be very special indeed. The friends I would make are still today my best friends, and the poetry we would write; well, I shall come to that soon, very soon.

4

A tragic verse brings joy to many hearts,
Enlightened poets toil with words of grief,
Delighting muses of the tragic arts,
But muses cruel will never lend relief,
Lest happiness should lend the poets rest,
And drawn are those who cannot write these songs,
To match their words and run the tragic test,
Inspired by nought to lay in verse life's wrongs,
These tuneless amateurs are verses' curse,
The truth of poets lies within their work,
The sweet lyred muse will tortured work emburse,
Inspiring tunes where tortured life does lurk.
The verse that lies untouched by thoughts divine,
Is verse not fed upon the muses' wine.

Original sin, you say? You wish me to speak of it?

"No, I simply mentioned that I shall have to talk about it at some point. Don't pester me muse. I have to continue now."

You mentioned it, not me.

"Because you spoke about the 'apple of your eye', that's why."

I was talking to the mermaids, not you, fool.

"O muse, we're reading each other's thoughts again."

They are *the same... why should we not live in a state of shared splendour?*

"I am not sure that there is much splendour about sharing anything with you, my friend. Why are you talking to the mermaids like that, anyway?"

It's part of my escape plan. I'm not going to tell you. You get on with the tale. That is your mission is it not O noble-minded husband?

"I intend to continue, thank you."

And stop talking to yourself.

"I'm not going to answer that."

...He was tricked you know?

"Who? What are you on about now?"

Satan, of course. He never fell from heaven. Who, in their right mind, except for maybe a pathetic fool like yourself, would fall from heaven? Come on, think about it. He was tricked.

"He was tricked?"

Yes, all part of his test, His test of original sin. Some sort of trapdoor on the path of heaven, I guess with a lure above it. Ahhh, the apple again. Not now my darlings, I'm talking. I'll come later.

"Muse, what are you talking about? Who are you talking to?"

It's the mermaids, Enchanting Melody and Siren Lure. We're becoming the best of friends. Don't worry about me, continue the hunt, dear poet. Let us battle again. As God and Satan once battled. How foolish! I loved you, dear poet, without your having to prove yourself. I did not tempt you to see if you met my standards. But He did! He made me test you. And, well, you made the deal with Him, not I. We'll see who writes the last verse yet.

I'm coming dears. These mermaids, you know, you should have spent more time with them. I can't believe you refused them... and for what?

The tale continues... the young poet arrives at a new home, yet again. The taxi disappears, like a ghost carriage into the night air which has just delivered the unknowing victim to the count's mansion. The poet stands on the pavement where he disembarked, studying the outline of his new home as it stands hauntingly in the dark. Darkness has the ability, do you not think, to make even the most sublime something have a certain menace to it? Then he enters the doors, rucksack-laden and a bag in each hand....

I wandered through school-like corridors, their walls displaying the remains of yesteryear's posters and notices whilst every now and then a new notice appears, announcing standards and directions or helpful hints and tips on 'how to survive further education'. This university would be my home for the next few years. Suddenly without warning, as I meandered slowly through, taking in my new surroundings and drifting past the smiling faces of my fellow lost souls, a strange voice ambushed me swiftly as a body followed it around the corner ahead.

"Hello, it's good to meet you, I'm the warden, my name is Colin. If you need anything, just let me know. Hmmm, don't appear to have your name down here, what did you say it was?" He knew full well I had as yet said nothing. This was obviously the tried and tested breaking line for his new wards. A difficult job, treating adults like adults in a childlike environment.

"Here it is, that's me," I pointed out my name on his list of newcomers.

"Okay, room A101. You think you can find it okay?"

"Don't worry, I'll be just fine. I'll follow these signs," I pointed.

The Stockford halls of residence for students was my abode for the first year of what were to be three memorable and extraordinary years of my life.

This place was to be a harvest ground for the muse, a birthplace for our creativity and a grave-yard for my soul. O yes, a certain part of it would die in this place along with my friend Erasmus Wallace, who did not praise folly; and also very nearly my second love, whose life I wished away one day because I felt that the love was not true and therefore would not last. I am sure that I was correct and sometimes these things happen, do they not? The problem with falling in love with a poet who is cursed by the muse is that emotions will often end in violence. How I regret the use of my powers and my vanity. Terrible muse, you that gave me these powers so great to turn the world and beat the heart. Why did you pick me upon which to feast your gut?

I soon arrived at my room, a small affair with the likeness of a cheap hostel. Nothing that a few selected wall decorations would not cure though. The first night I met a few new friends, people who had arrived before me or who were arriving now. The first introductions were basic and friendly; everyone wanted to get on in their new world, of course. The following day I did not need to register or report. It was a free day, a chance to explore and to lay foundations. So I walked, alone in the morning and with a friend in the afternoon, and I set out to discover this new place. I found that this quiet university in the countryside replaced stormy cliffs with beautiful gardens, full of swaying trees and fine flowers. Scientifically enhanced and monitored ponds stretched out at the edges of the campus, with small waterfalls at intervals singing their continuous tunes, and these ponds supplied banks of grass upon which I would lay in the summer and soak up the warm sun. It is peculiar how the same sun does not shine the same in different places.

In the afternoon I walked with a friend to a local pub by the river, a long walk but a fine one since the pub's excellent reputation was well-deserved and it rewarded our efforts with good food and an envied atmosphere. My friend, in fact an old acquaintance from my school at home, had also found respite at this university. However, we progressed our friendship at this place little further, being in different halls and wishing to make new starts, the both of us.

After a fair and enjoyable day I returned back to my room. People were still arriving from various parts and setting up their own little private dwellings where they would hide from the rest of the world when things were tough, or where they would sit with others over late night coffee and put the world to their satisfaction. I went to my own little room and continued my own preparations.

That night I dreamt. I dreamt that I flew upon similar paths to those I had walked upon during the morning hours. I flew low and fast across the ponds and through the trees. I heard the scurrying of frightened animals in my dream. I know now that I was dreaming the perversion of the muse as it sought out its new home and found a substitute for the broken rocks and the battering sea. Where, it must have wondered, would it find the inspiration with which to feed me in order to gorge itself? O yes, and where, it wondered, would it find the souls upon which it would feed? The muse flew high and wide and searched not only the land but the future also. Love it would give me, with friends it would supply me and then tragedy it would inflict upon me, for that is the nature and the gift of the muse. Yes, yes, that is how I spent my first two days in this new place.

~

I suppose that I would have preferred at that stage of my life to have dwelt in the tragedy of my broken heart upon the night-time cliffs of my home, alone. The muse would have found its fill there, I am sure of it. But, that frightful spirit intended the situation to become much worse. Her belly, unable to be filled, required more than a broken heart, it demanded a battered soul. And that is why I found myself in this place of learning, this place of idle minds embroiled deep in philosophy, for philosophy suits the idle mind. My room at Stockford soon became full of books, some read and bent, some in waiting and gleaming still. Their pages filled the room with an aroma of relaxing study and glorious snoozes, those snoozes where the words on the pages mingle together and run around like little animals whilst the book becomes heavier and heavier until, 'thud', it falls from the bed and wakes up the tired reader. The titles of these books were such that had interested me as a child and were familiar to my studies so far. My area of expertise was to be ancient magic, coupled with the mysteries of Renaissance literature wherever it had found a foothold in magic and the supernatural. Ancient Greek, philosophy, religion and literature were all to play their part. They supplied a strong founding which slanted my mind to favour the muse's style, such that it was. I do not really know if this was part of the muse's plan. I doubt it since I enjoyed this part of it, but nonetheless, it was attractive to the playful spirit, obviously reminding her of the ancients who recognised these devils enough to give them names. Names so that we may label their characters and know which one is haunting us at any time.

After a few more days settling in, I discovered the delights of a university library. The creaky doors of the old library led to a three storey building, the lowest of which was underground. This was a place of archives and empty shelves, endless stacks and but a few students either seeking solace from the masses or researching from an old text, unwanted in the main library. This was my favourite library, a place where I too could feel unwanted but secure. I loved the age of the books and the quietness of the place. It appealed to my nature, I believe, though perhaps the muse was the attracted party, dragging my soul beside it. The new library carried the weight of knowledge. Knowledge and understanding, such an essential part of society. Each book-case was a temptation, a lesson waiting to be learned with unknown results. O muse, how I still feel you there each time I go, whether it be the old library of that place in the country or the small library in my own home. How I can smell you in the old pages and see your reflection in the swollen glass of the windows. Do you have a brother hiding there to watch me, I wonder?

I also made friends, lots of them, though just a few good friends, as is the case with all, I suppose. On my floor in Stockford there were three girls who, from their first encounter, became social triplets, a nucleus of laughter and welcome. Their names were Amber, Scarlet and Jade. In the end Scarlet would stay here to continue her studies, long after we all had left, Amber would meet her destiny in the limbo of a dreadful not-world until I could rescue her, and Jade would leave and head off to... I do not know to where. The three of them were almost inseparable... almost. Amber was in a couple of my classes and so we soon found a link in this common factor and we became good friends, we made each other laugh. Yes, how we made each other laugh. Amber brought my life back on track as befitted me, more conventionally. We played silly games together, we drank until we couldn't drink any more and we learnt together to measure life moment by moment.

Another from my course was the famous and fated Erasmus

Wallace. Famous because I have mentioned the man already, and fated because, well, that was his fate, to be so. Erasmus I first met in one of our professors' study rooms. We had arrived at the same time, in order to sign up for a particular course, but I do not remember exactly which one it was. His voice was meaningful and wise. He was older than I and had obviously not come here straight from school. When we discovered that we would be studying together over the next three years, we cemented the foundations of this relationship by strolling together to the coffee bar. We found that we had similar characters in many ways and not so in many ways also. My strange and supernatural background, about which I am telling you, had not really materialised itself fully and I was consequently unaware of the full realisation of what my life was like. Erasmus seemed to have been shown a taste of the workings making up his, also strange, existence. And the two of us quietly chatted together and worked each other out as best we could, both of us realising, without necessarily knowing it, that we were fighting similar battles and would end up finding similar defeats at the hands of life.

The third of my very good friends was Mercy Marriette. She was another poet's tragedy, she was another muse's saviour and I was the friend who would always be there to hear her stories of love and tragedy. I believe she had her own quiet muse sitting there on her shoulder. I am grateful that it was not the callous and dread muse which adorned me. Often we would speak together of stories of love, of hate and of tragedy. The four of us, Mercy, Erasmus, myself and also my love to be – Amber, made excellent friends. Mercy was a perfect friend to me, though the relationship was different since she was too beautiful for the muse not to be stirring in her passions and thinking of the two of us entwined upon a bed of thorns. And why not, since the tragedy of the triangle would have suited the playful muse perfectly. She had planned so well the intricate web of my friendships with these three. So manipulative in her scheming, that playful muse enjoyed the bed of thorns which she made for all of us. How appropriate to feed her thirst for blood.

The same was in fact true of my relationship with Erasmus; he was too good a friend to me and hence another target for the muse, though in a different way.

Mercy was not on my course, but Erasmus knew her from his hall and that is how we had met. Not being on our course we saw less of her than we would have liked and often it was myself, Erasmus and Amber who met and discussed life over a coffee or two after a seminar or lecture. We would often meet up with Mercy in the evenings though she also much enjoyed her own company.

As we all became firmer and firmer friends, we lived our time at this place exploring a strange new world which at one time I would have considered impossible and make-believe, but which I now know to be the fateful and supernatural world of the muse, who controlled my nearly-every sentence and my nearly-every emotion. However, I must now continue the tale and tell you how we came to understand the role of the muse more fully at this place and how she manipulated the most sacred of feelings in order to quench this blood-thirst for tragedy. Look, now I repeat myself and she will grow weary of my tale if I do not come soon to her role. I would not want you to lose your interest, dear muse.

~

The days catalogued themselves into weeks and this new place grew rapidly familiar. Friends settled and life seemed to slot into place. The winter would be coming soon. My studies were introduced slowly. The subject was one upon which I had barely touched at school, though I had found interesting the many books on the matter which I had read in the spare time of my youth. Erasmus had studied the subject in more depth than I, and his ideas were creative and original. We worked well together, he enjoyed teaching me what he knew of the ancient magical papyri and the associated texts. My knowledge of the Renaissance period exceeded his and we complemented each other at our work. Amber enjoyed our discussions also and the three of us became close. Our lecturers were an odd bunch, understandably. I, for one, and I know Amber also, were here because we wanted to come to university to study but we had chosen courses we enjoyed rather than courses which would benefit us in a career. I wonder how we stacked up morally against the other students? There were those who had chosen subjects with a future, but who had no intention of pursuing that future and little did they seem to enjoy their work. There were those who tried and would fail at their chosen careers, and there were a few who benefited from their studies to apply these benefits to their jobs. The three of us benefited greatly from our work, though none of us became like our lecturers. Professor 'Distinguished Idealist' was their leader. He had studied pure Classics and knew little of life outside the walls of a university or an ancient ruin. His appearance said as much as his personality in this respect. Our main contact was Doctor Neam who specialised in occult texts and their transition through the Middle Ages. The actual course we were studying was a relatively new one; it used to be the preserve of PhD students or those studying for a Masters degree. This was only the second year we lowly undergraduates had been accepted for the course. Our lecturers, as I have said, were generally odd, at first. Their dedication throughout their lives to this subject and the fact that they had made these studies their living had cast them in such a stereotype that it really did take some time to get to know them and to brush away the dust of their unusualness. And this was the setting in which the muse and I found ourselves.

I don't think that any of them, the tutors I mean, recognised the muse. Their eyes were fixed for reading and thinking, not adjusted to see the true reality of the supernatural. But there was one girl in some of our classes, the wise but not liked Anne Black, who was studying the witch trials of the Middle Ages, whom I sensed stared at me sometimes, focusing just off from my eyes. I cannot be sure since at the time I had no reason to notice anything and the stare would have seemed that of a person in deep thought, an idle minded philosopher. Looking back, I believe she saw something because one night she ran naked through the campus of the university screaming and raving. She was discovered the next morning, foam frozen at her mouth and her little body scratched from bushes and cold through to the bone. I remember that it had been cold that night, but it did not freeze, and her death was something of a mystery. Also, it was the last, and fortunately only time, that any other person tried to stand between myself and my tragic fate, and for this reason, among others, I believe that she was among the first to see the true appearance of my muse. Oh yes, how I remember that night with all of its terror and foiled plots and messy deaths. But, this story I shall come to, soon.

5

The first term finished quickly, each lasting less than three months with generous holidays dividing them. During my first break, that Christmas, I returned home to see my family. My father's business was doing very well by now and he could afford to spend more time away from work. My brother was working as a mechanic, and a good trade of failed engines and rusty body-work kept him busy. My sister had left home and was living with her boyfriend, near our old home. We had all suspected that she would return one day, she had never been keen on the move.

"I'm glad to hear that things are going well for you, son," my father would often say. "But what will you do with that blasted degree when you get back?" He would have preferred I do something with a financially rewarding future.

"There are lots of things I could do", it was the truth. "I could teach, I could research for a museum, I could write." Yes, that was what I really wanted to do and I needed such a background to prepare myself, to nurture my style and to gather material. But that is difficult to explain, especially to one's own parent who has given so much to get his children this far in life, only to see them sit back and relax for further education at the prime of their working life. I don't think he understood and that is what made him even more special, that he trusted my decision and supported my chosen path. My mother had simply been determined for me to go to university and had put little further thought into it. She assumed that all graduates would lead stable and rewarding lives. Not true, mum. But anyway, don't worry about it, I'll manage...

"I'll probably do a mixture of these sorts of jobs, I'm not sure, I'll see what's available when I leave. But I do realise that I'm lucky, so don't worry."

Christmas was good that year. I was spoiled by a mother who had missed me and a cat that had been sleeping in the kitchen each night instead of the comfort of my room. It snowed briefly on Christmas Eve, a light flurry. At the time I was sitting watching the moon reflecting in the sea. Clouds brushed passed it, herded by the chill wind. It was cold and I did not stay for long, but I had so wanted to see again the beaches where we had played and loved and fought and lost, those few years ago. I so wanted to sit and talk with Autumn, in the light of the moon, and ask her what went wrong, to tell her I loved her, to tell her I hated her. I could feel the pain still teasing at my heart. But, memories eased the remaining pain and I thought that it would be nice to ease it further by capturing those memories, in verse. But I was not quite in the mood for writing. My time would come, and so I returned home to bed and to Christmas morning.

Do not bother them with Christmas, poet. Go straight to the next term and that wonderful spring when love unsung was born.

"Indeed, you are right, but what of the first time I saw the mermaid, on the last day of this holiday as I walked with my father on the cliffs?"

So you've finally come to terms with that first sighting: how you dispelled it at the time, though.

"Of course, that was different, it's always harder to believe the first time."

Allow me, for I was there calling them. It was a fine day for a walk, oh yes your father enjoyed his walks along the cliffs. But he never ventured as far down the cliffs as you, at least not until that one fateful day. You walked and talked, and talked and walked, "what's that place?" he said, pointing. "It's Thompson's

Bay," you said. "Named after the late and mythological Captain Thompson" you explained, "it is said that he smuggled goods into the bay but was taken by a hideous storm one night which crashed him hard against the rocks. His body was never found, though they did not search all of the many caves in the bay, so it is said." A fine tale that you recited, learned from your school days I guess, before my time. "Is that someone swimming down there, son? The water must be cold, don't you think? Is it someone?" Of course, dear father of my poet, it is my mermaid friend, one of those fiends who now taunt me. And I know that you saw her, poet, though you pretended that it was not what you saw, you denied your beloved fantasy. "I suppose I'll take a stroll down there one afternoon, get the old legs going won't it?" Oh, how I laughed, poet, when the old man said that. It certainly did get the old legs going, I recall them struggling at the loose rock as he slipped nearer the sea. The look in his eyes as he turned. Yes, it is better I tell the tale, poet, you were not even there. Scream he did, yes, screaming he fell into the icy water, my cold hands upon his ankles dragging him down, further and further. And to where? I'll tell you to where, dear reader; into the very vial from which I had come. And how, you ask, did it come to be there? Our dear poet had left it there, full of hate and anger, had left it there full of disappointment, had left it there for his father. My task was easy, I fulfilled the wish of the poet, I simply finished what you had started.

And here he lies, dear poet, in his little vial, right here in my hand. Ha, ha ha.

"Enough, you have spoken, muse. You have spoken also of your own fate, trapped as you are in the deep sea-cave. Your words sting me with lies and deception. I did not place the vial as a trap, I threw it in anger, into the ocean, hoping it would crack the head of the mermaid I thought I saw there gliding in the shadows of the coughing sea."

Oh yes, that mermaid, you were right, I placed her there once more, a shadow beneath the waves. So like your father's lover, was she not? And so similar, both of them secrets to the world and seen only by you. How did you feel, tell me again, when you watched in your mind what you could not believe, your father and another woman, a not-mother? How did it feel? O I remember the pain and I had seen it before you, knowing how it would hurt you.

"You are the culprit, muse."

Not I, this whole affair was long before my release. I did not fill the vial with hate, you did. You threw the vial at the mermaid fair and she read your wish, read your hate. I was simply a catalyst for your own desire. And look how you have rewarded me, stuck as I am in this deep sea-cave.

"You are stuck, well and fast I hope, muse. But this tragedy is to occur much later on in the story, dear muse, so do not rush me now to tell this tale. My father's body sits still in his bed, his tongue mostly silent, his head usually drooped and his eyes often glazed. A body that functions without a soul is but little body at all and no life for any man. I know that the mermaids have his soul in their deep sea-cave. But, it is a price I can live with for now, as long as I know that you are trapped beside him. One day I shall discover his caged soul on the beach as I discovered yours, and I shall release him from his pain."

O poet, how ideal your words from one who is such a conformist. Everything you and I could have shared together, yet you threw me aside and cast me to the ocean deep. O but I suppose that I shall yet surprise you.

"That would not surprise me. And now that you have spoken your piece I shall continue the tale. I think perhaps you have grown strong from your speech, I shall subdue you with some tragedy which you can no longer have."

Subdue me, poet, subdue away, for I love to hear your fine tongue spin our tale.

"Noble to the last, dear muse. Why can I not hate you without loving you also…?"

Because? Just, because. Now it is late poet, sing us to sleep and continue tomorrow.

"What shall I sing?"

Sing of true love…

Should roses carry thorns upon their stem,
While other flowers wear an easier veil?
Should mountains cover Earth's most precious gem,
When sifting shallow streams will rarely fail?
Perhaps a sign, for those who roses mind,
That beauteous form will often danger shape,
Or warning dire, for those who diamonds find,
That trembling caves may threaten their escape.
Yet know a meaning more than omens few,
And reason that the pain in love's desire
Contrives assurance for the suitor true:
The purest tune demands the dearest lyre.
Should roses carry thorns upon their stem?
For truest love my soul I would condemn.

"Now sleep, dear muse, and dream, dream…"

Good night, poet.

"Good night, my muse."

6

"Love is in the air," they have sung. I should tell them that it is not only in the air, it is in the wind, the water, the blood, the dreams, the hate, the passion; it is everywhere and there are none who can hide from it. Cursed, wretched love, how graceful and beautiful you are.

The first spring of my first year, that is where we want to be.

Work and university life was progressing well. We were looking to move away from halls the next year and into a house, which would require a few of us to share. About five would seem a good number. It seemed certain that Erasmus and myself and Amber would be a central group, and we needed a couple of others to join us, depending on the exact state of the place we would find to rent. As it transpired, there were to be five of us, Jade and Scarlet making up the quintet. This was not such a surprise to me. I had considered that this would be a fair plan earlier during this term and to concrete this we indeed found a fine place that we could move into next autumn; we reserved this with a deposit and our next year was looking to be good.

Our prompt success was admired by others in the same situation and some asked us for help, since we had seen a few different places in our search and knew what was around. Mercy had agreed for Scarlet to drive her to a few places. She was looking to share a house with some of her friends from her course. Scarlet was the only one among us with a car at university; she was in popular demand because of it. The day they were supposed to go

Scarlet was sick with fever, and I was asked to play chauffeur.

"Okay, next stop is Titchworth Avenue, it says here 'a four-bedroom terrace'. Sound okay?"

"I wish I could have something away in the country. A little farmhouse, all to myself, with a chimney and ivy growing on the walls."

"And a dog?"

"Yes, and a dog." She giggled, completing the fantasy.

"Well, how would you get to campus?" I asked.

"Oh, I wouldn't go, except maybe once a month to check my work with my handsome professor. I'd be a writer and keep myself elusive and mysterious. A recluse. Inspiring, no?"

"You need inspiration, and I agree, away from others is best. Down by the sea, that's where I would go." I didn't intend to give the game away, that I too would like to be a writer.

"You like writing too? I didn't know you lived near the sea. Do you go there from here, it's not far?"

"It's far enough, and I get enough of it when I'm at home."

"Oooh, that sounds painful, want to tell me about her?"

I smiled and looked at her while we drove. She was looking at me, her bright eyes beckoning for a story of romance and broken hearts.

"You're very clever. Do you have such a similar story that you recognise mine?"

"You're very clever too. But, I don't know that we have time to talk about it all now. After this I'll buy you a cheeseburger and a coffee, I know that you and Erasmus have a passion for them."

"That's true, but I like the cheeseburger and he likes the coffee. I'll settle for fish and chips and a bottle of wine though."

"Done. Look, here we are, Titchworth Avenue."

We soon finished, Mercy made a deal on the house we saw after the one in Titchworth Avenue. It was fair and reasonably priced and she'd be happy there. She was sharing with a couple from her course and another single girl. She was happier with this situation than sharing with us. She preferred to be able to get away from everyone at a moment's notice and these friends suited her better than we did for this purpose. The others were all older than she was and from similar backgrounds; they would get on well together. Mercy insisted that she would buy the fish and chips and I insisted that I buy the wine. I had returned Scarlet's car and we walked to Mercy's halls to eat and to meet Erasmus. When we arrived there was no Erasmus to be found and a party of drunken stupor had evolved amongst the students in the kitchen. Thus we took refuge in Mercy's room to eat, drink and talk.

"It was really kind of you to drive me around today."

"You are most welcome."

"You remember that night a couple of months ago when we drove with Erasmus and Scarlet to the countryside, to the old druid's top stone? That's what they call it, yes?"

"Yeah, that's the one, the night Amber was with us as well, you mean?" There had been several occasions when we had been out to the countryside at night. It was great to go running up the steep hillsides and through the glades at night-time. There were a few huge, odd shaped stones that looked like sacrificial altars to the untrained eye, and a couple of places we had found in the woods, clearings where one night we had made a fire and tried to frighten each other with ghost stories. Sometimes we'd even get up early and go and watch the dawn, or, if we couldn't face the demanding rise at that hour, we would squeeze into Scarlet's car and go and watch the sunset instead. Both were very beautiful. The area was one of quite important significance and many odd looking tourists could be seen wandering through the woods during the dawn. I do not know whether they were '*want to be*' druids invoking the sun to rise, amazed each day at their own success, or just other poets looking for romance and solitude among the trees. It was a good place to be and we knew we were lucky to be so near a special place like this.

"I think she likes you, you know?"

"Amber? I don't think so. There's not that much to like. But we get on well together. She's a good friend." I didn't feel uncomfortable with the question. Many people had joked about our relationship, how well we made each other laugh. But, I was sure that we were not fated to be together unless it was to make each other laugh, and I believe I can say that this gives little scope for love, which is too complicated for laughter.

"Don't worry, I'm just teasing you. I know that you take love seriously, that's why I feel relaxed around you. You wouldn't believe how many friends I've lost, or thought I had, but never really did? All those idiots who let you down or just pester you like drunken apes? Sorry, am I going on?"

She was on a little bit of a crusade, but I was still listening and felt almost glad that my experiences had made me the person I was, someone who took love seriously. No more would I fall for someone who could not return the feeling. But I know that should my precious Autumn have walked through that door just at that moment I would have taken her strongly in my arms and never let her go again.

We carried on talking for a couple of hours and we whiled away the time with stories of each other's painful past lives. We exchanged personal memories. We managed, for my part at least, to make it sound a lot more dramatic than it actually had been, perhaps the wine was helping. When I got up to leave she tapped my shoulder in a friendly manner, as Amber would have done, and said, "I hope you don't change, you're a nice guy." I wasn't sure if this would do me any good in life, but it helped at that time. The person that Autumn had made me was suddenly someone whom I found I liked. But why would I change? Did she know something more about me, or about men, than I did? Probably, but I was determined not to change, if this was the way people I respected liked me.

As I walked back I smiled. I was happy. It had been a good evening. I felt happy with life.

That night, curled up in my warm bed, I dreamt: *I awoke at the window of my bedroom, looking out at the gardens. I looked below, the gardens were moving beneath me, I was flying with the night breeze. I rolled and glided through the moonlit air, it was fantastic. I flew high, I could see the valleys where we visited sometimes. My body took me toward the woods, not where we used to go, but a different glade. Suddenly I descended, quickly. I was frightened. I flew through the trees, scraping some and twisting painfully around others. Then I stopped. It was misty. A body lay sitting up against a tree and another, taller than is natural, stood in front of me. I looked at the body slumped by the tree. It was a lifeless Amber, her flesh white and her mouth hung open in dumb horror. I could feel my heart beating more and more quickly, I turned at a voice, a groan, from the other, tall figure. I realised then that it wasn't a tall person. It was a body suspended from a tree, and its head, was high as mine as I floated in the air. I looked closer as its eyes swung down towards my gaze. O horror, my friend Erasmus hanging from a tree by his neck, pain and shock etched onto his face as he muttered his last words which were inaudible to me. Horror. I awoke. Mercy was leaning over my bed, soothing me from a nightmare, cuddling me with gentle words and sounds. She spoke 'look it's okay, here she is, they're both right here.' She placed a ring on my finger. She kissed my cheek. She faded away. So beautiful she was, in my dream, even more so than normal.*

As she faded, beauty into darkness, another figure developed from where she had been. It was a tall figure, bedraggled in dress and charactered with a huge bushy beard to which birds clung and chirped happily. The face was old but I recognised it. "You" I spoke in my dream, "where have you been?" "I have been watching you, my brother, for all of these years, watching and waiting and waiting and watching, my little lost brother, but you can now call me Old Jack, for I am still the protector of your dreams and your guardian." Old Jack, as my not-brother would now be known, wore feathers in his hair and his cheeks sparkled with diamonds streaming from his eyes. "You have been gone for so long, where have you been?" Fog drifted around me and clawed at my feet. I looked up to hear from my not-brother. "I must go now, I have been gone, I have aged so many years, I have been gone, little man, away from here in my own world, little man; take good care now and watch the fog, look how it creeps upon you like a wolf." I was caught in a blanket of fog, struggling to reach out to Old Jack who faded as my eyes were shrouded. "Old Jack, Old Jack." The fog drowned my voice and poured through my open mouth into panicking lungs where I felt it chill and turn into liquid. My vision returned and I saw water around me. I was sitting on a rock at the bottom of the ocean kicking at the sand like a bored child waiting for his friends to arrive. I carried the sad weight of a restless head upon one arm and fidgeted at some seaweed with the other. There was a tap on my shoulder. I turned to see nothing, only the sound of laughter met my ears. "Pesky mermaids" I spoke. "Hello, what are you doing here?" The voice was that of my father but the body that spoke I recognised as Erasmus. "I'm waiting to play, isn't it obvious?" "But you can't play" was the reply, "you must write the verse, that is your fate." "I don't understand." I didn't understand, at the time. Then my friend's body was still and became lifeless in front of my eyes. His eyes turned white and his flesh pale. "No, no!" I yelled, but no sound delivered. More laughter, more anonymous taps, more and more seaweed suddenly around me, tightening, smothering me. I yelled... yelled!!!

I awoke. It was an incredibly vivid dream, I can recall it so well. I was sweating so much. I sat up. I went immediately to the telephone downstairs and called Erasmus, to check he was okay. After a few minutes of ringing he answered the phone. That was no surprise. At four in the morning he would often be awake, still studying while the other students slept. Of course it would be him that answered the phone; he was alive, at least. I was relieved to hear his voice and explained the dream to him. He laughed it off, "too much Arcana Mundi," he said. But as I spoke to him I noticed something strange. A ring had been placed upon my finger as I slept. I never wore jewellery. I didn't have any such ring. It was the ring from the dream. She who comforted me from the nightmare had left me the ring, *'look it's okay, they're both right here…'* she had said. The ring was of old silver metal with a dull amber stone centered. A dull, amber stone… Once more, the relics of my life were manifesting themselves to me, as they had done in my youth. The ring would find its place, unspoken, in my drawer at home, with the rest of my youthful relics. I returned to bed. I was shivering with cold now, though my right shoulder was warm. I told no one about the ring upon my finger.

~

"O muse, spring is in the air, is it not, and the end of the tale is now in sight?"

True, true…No. Rubbish, what am I saying? There is much to say before the forest glade and the magic spun therein, you and your stupid spells, and you call me a primitive spirit.

"Yes. I am getting ahead of myself."

Getting excited, more like. Spring is in the air indeed. I am stuck in here, fated to a thousand years of Divine Retribution and her pals singing old sailor songs and shanties to me and dancing with rotting corpses. Do me some justice and don't check me out before I'm due. Now get on with it, and put some heroism into it, boy, I am famous, if you will recall.

"I shall continue."

What about the mermaid story?

"You'd like the mermaid story?"

Yes, please.

"Okay. I'll tell it to you to keep you happy. It was a bright spring day. Mercy sat studying by the little ponds at the edge of the campus, where the scientific ecosystems were being created. Little fish catalogued and sorted lived alongside ducks and frogs and other assorted and numbered animals. A little experiment to harvest data. For me, the experiment afforded some comfortable banks of grass overlooking the endless streams and ponds, numbered though they were. The data and the reasoning behind the nature here did not really interest me. It was just a good place to study, or to sit and relax. I had seen Mercy sitting in the distance and went up to her. I knew that she would be there, though. Do you recall so far muse?"

Every step, every sound, every half writ verse, go on, dear boy, go on.

'May I join you?'

'Of course, I was about to take a break from this rubbish anyway,' she said.

'You're going somewhere now?'

'No, I mean I was about to stop reading. I could sit here for hours. Stay with me.'

'I love it here too, it's very quiet.' I sat down beside her and reclined comfortably on one elbow to face her.

'Peaceful.'

'I guess.'

'Creative.'

'I suppose. Are you creating anything?'

'No. But you create something for me. Will you?' She asked.

'What?'

'Hmmm. Tell me a story. Tell me a story about the sea.'

"She lay back and blew her hair from her eyes, shut as they were against the sun. Do you recall muse? Do you recall?"

Oh, do go on. Don't worry about me, I recall, I recall, now tell me, tell me, your words, not mine.

'Do you believe in mermaids?"

Silence.

I brushed her face with a winter-killed, lifeless leaf from the fresh green grass. 'Oh sweetness,' I said sarcastically, 'do you believe in mermaids?'

'Of course I do,' she claimed.

'Do you know how a mermaid is born?'

'Tell me,' she didn't really know the truth.

'There is an old king of the sea who lives underneath the continent of Africa in the deepest of deep-sea caves. There he dwells in the fiery cave, surrounded by tools and recipes of creation. He creates all of the fish in the sea, the whales, the dolphins, the lobsters and the sharks. He blows and coughs from out of his deepest of deep sea-caves when he wants there to be a storm, and the tides move up and down with his breath. He has a long, white, old beard, full of sunken ships and treasure which litters the floor of his deepest of deep-sea caves. And he also listens to the tunes in the hearts of men and the hearts of women who roam upon the land. He hears their music through the chimes of the sea gulls and the flying birds which tell him of the world above. And every time he hears word of a man falling in love with a woman, he creates a mermaid in the likeness of that woman so that she may roam free in the seas. And then if the man is too shy to tell that woman that he is in love with her, he will find the mermaid, if his love is true, of course. Because he will sit above the cliffs and stare out to sea and call her name, the name of the love to whom he never dared confess. If his love is true then the mermaid will come for him and take him down to the depths of the ocean floor, where they will make love among the sunken wrecks and husbands lost at sea. And after they have loved they will both disappear and be no more, except happy in each other's arms. And if the love is not true… Well, then the mermaid will not come for that soul, but instead she will roam the seas, free to live as she pleases, and these are the mermaids that we often see; they are the lies of men who do not know their own hearts.'

'And if the man overcomes his shyness and tells the woman he loves her ?' She asked me.

'Then the mermaid is doomed to die a watery death as he whispers the words into his love's ear, torn apart as she is from a broken heart. Unless of course the woman rejects her suitor's love, in which case the mermaid comes painfully upon the dry land in the dark hours and seeks out the woman to tell her of her wrongs; that is if the love is true, of course.'

'The mermaids can tell?'

'Oh yes, they can tell. But the old king of the sea cannot tell, that is why he creates the mermaids. Do you understand now?'

'Let's go for a coffee.'

'Okay, let's go.'

Beautiful, beautiful story and so true, as though I whispered the words into your mind as you spoke.

"Now I have told you the story, are you happy, muse?"

Very much so, dear poet, very much so; just as I recall, the exact very way it did occur.

"Good, now shall we proceed?"

Yes, I shall remain untroubling to you, let us go on.

"Fine, now let me see… ah, yes, the poem in the library, that will suffice next. A little interlude, muse, before I come back to you to continue this thing."

~

The next day I sat in the library, my head in one hand and a busy pencil in the other. I was thinking about the dream and doodling my thoughts into some unknown indecipherable symbols, common among many a schoolboy's papers. I started to write. I scribbled short and long symbols at the top of the page, a U followed by a dash, five pairs of them, to set an iambic pentameter. By the time the poem is finished the bar will be covered with dots, the echoes of words to test their scansion. Down the side of the page, there were fourteen letters I placed: ABABCDCDEFEFGG. This would set my rhyme and form the discipline to which poetry should comply. Poetry should not just be the instant frolics of an imaginative mind, churning out the scenic beauty of passionate appeal. Poetry must be set according to form, only then will the true verse, as it was intended by the muse, come forth. Don't think that we humans write the verses ourselves, oh no. They are written for us and our lives wrapped around them. Only by the formulaic spell of the set verse are we able to cast the words from the spirit world and watch them manifest on the page, where they will stay forever, testimony to our pain. O beautiful poetry.

I placed a line. I tried to imagine some stirring feelings at the same time. I must not love, she who must not be loved. But yet I could be her hero. Yes, this was a fine theme upon which to write – imagine a hero who cannot speak his love to a princess who would never listen. How tragic a fate for man. *The saving of your soul would be my task, A task to which I'd dedicate my life.* Yes, yes, that's it. But, I must retain my distance, for she loves the comfortable distance, *Your foes, with sword I'd cut, and slash with knife, But know me not for I should wear a mask, My name I'll keep, so do not think to ask.* Well, maybe there's something there. I'd have to finish this later, perhaps it was not quite ready. Although, *For beauty such as yours would ne'er be mine...* The feelings I created I needed to feel in my own heart – I had to borrow the hearts of those around me, my friends and my loves – I had to cannibalise their own hearts so that I could borrow their pain and their suffering to create my own tragedy and fill the heart of the muse.

"What are you doing?"

"If not I'd fought, my court you would decline." I was looking at Amber. She had seen me sitting in the library and had decided to interrupt my study with the temptation of a stroll down to the town and a coffee by the cathedral.

"What?"

"Coffee?"

"That's what I do here."

"Okay, let's go."

We sat and drank and ate ice cream for the rest of the afternoon. We spoke mainly of the new house and how great next year would be. It was a good afternoon and in the evening we passed by Erasmus' room to see if he was there. It was almost time for the Easter holidays. Home again we would all troop, to our families.

"No, I'm staying here this holiday."

"Why?" I asked Erasmus. "You're going to study?"

"Yeah, and besides, I can't stand Easter, my sister comes down and visits and she's got screaming kids. The whole house is a mess when she's there. I'll be better off here."

"Fine, if you'll be okay."

We were all quiet, it had been a long day and Amber wanted to go home.

"I'll walk you, let's go. Hey, old man. I'll come round tomorrow, we'll go for coffee and a walk down by the river. Are you working all night?"

"With such an offer, I shall work only half the night and sleep the rest so that I'm all yours."

"Okay I'll see you then. 'Night."

"See you both later."

We walked home together, Amber and I. I kept thinking of the dream and I wondered why I had dreamt of the cold and still Amber against the tree. When we reached the door of our halls I looked at her, closely in her eyes, "If dreamers love do in their deep sleep find, And lovers dream of loving when they wake, Then let me sleep within my heart and mind, With dreams so real that dreaming lovers make."

She stared back at me in the buzzing light of the door-way lamp. "Shakespeare?"

"Oh, no. Nothing like it. An old, old forgotten poet. You wouldn't have heard of him."

"Oh, well. A drink?"

"A quick one."

We ventured inside to the kitchen on our floor, quietly in case some of the others were asleep. No such luck, our quiet coffee to be would be accompanied by the very hospitable Jade and the excitable Scarlet, which was fine, but also paying a visit was the annoying and boisterous Burton Rogers who, everyone knew, had taken a fancy to the unreceptive Amber. "Hello Burton", I spoke up, "you been waiting up for me?"

"Not quite, I was just passing by; I brought back some books I'd borrowed from Jade. I hear you guys are all sharing a house next year."

"That's right, what are you up to?" There was a trace of dangerous teasing in Scarlet's voice.

"Not decided yet, I'll probably get something sorted out with a few friends of mine."

"Good, who would that be?" mocked Jade.

"Not sure yet."

The girls allowed there to be an embarrassing silence.

"I think I'll go now." It was a relief, he wasn't a particularly likeable person, by his own doing. He was sometimes foul mouthed, turned up at annoying times and did not know when to be discreet. We thought we'd be a little naughty as he left for his room on the floor below. He made his good nights and dwelt on Amber's look as she bid him the same. This firmed her resolve to take action, just for fun of course.

"Come with me," Scarlet said cheekily, we thought we knew what she had in mind as she picked up a few newspapers and some sticky tape.

We crept down to his room once we knew he was inside and taped newspaper up across the frame of his door, wallpapering him in to his room.

"It's not that funny you know, we need a little more humour in it," Jade whispered, thinking hard for what she could add. "Hold on." She disappeared upstairs and returned a few minutes later with some matches and some glue. Meanwhile we had joked in near silence listening to the odd sounds and movements from within the room, knowing that at any moment we could be discovered. Other members of this floor passed us by in the corridor outside the room, barely noting our presence, probably used to such goings-on, such was the nature of this lifestyle. Jade carefully sought out the artist and designer in her and glued the match box sideways up to the floor at the edge of the newspaper. A match positioned on the striking side of the box and levered with a makeshift pivot. "This isn't going to work Jade, sweety," spoke the more bold Scarlet. "Hold on, and get ready to run."

We looked at each other contently. I suppose moments like this were indeed what being young was all about, a good bonding experience as parents or office managers would like to call it. I looked at Amber, she looked at me, Scarlet leant down and looked at us both. Scarlet then took the matches, box and stick, "look, if you do it like this it will work a lot... better." Her last pair of words were accompanied with a flaring noise and a promising glow as she lit the match and touched the paper barricade.

"Darling, shall I?" Amber whispered to me.

"You sound great when you whisper, you know that?" I nodded.

"Oh, Burton dear, let me in, I want to see you." She swooned at his door. We ran, quietly, and the sound of feet leaping from their bed and scurrying across the floor faded inaudibly. We turned to see a rather nice, though short-lived, inferno creep up from the foot of the door as a fiery tempered Burton stamped and kicked through the burning barricade. "You bloody girls, I'll get you," was the last we heard that night. We knew that he wouldn't venture further that night. It was more his style to forget it now and soothe his wounded pride with oblivion. Amber grabbed my hand and pulled me up the stairs. "We'd better get to our own rooms now, in case he comes up." She kissed me on the cheek and turned for her place. The others fled quicker to theirs and I was left alone to saunter to my own refuge and hope indeed that the comical Burton Rogers remained un-vengeful.

"Good night, I had a nice day," I said quietly to my friends even though they had each locked themselves away already.

The scenes were being written by my dear muse. Slowly and purposefully the relationships developed and plotted, all of them building to that final moment, that terrible moment which, my reader friend, you must ensure never happens to you.

~

That night I dreamt again of Old Jack, my friend and protector, my lost not-brother who was in fact no longer my not-brother but a different being within my imagination. 'Jack, Jack, what are you doing? What's that noise?' I could see him from around a corner in the corridor of our halls. He was making a banging noise rhythmically: boom, boom, boom. I moved around the corner and stood aghast at his actions when I saw the extent of the scene. He held the bloody corpse of Burton Rogers in one hand and pounded its pulped head against a reddened wall. Bits fell off from the corpse as he did so. 'Jack, Jack, what are you doing? Stop.' He stopped, and turned slowly to look at me. He spoke in a deep tone, slowly and without good clarity. 'This is not supposed to be, this thing and your Amber. This is not meant to be. This thing not meant to stand in your way.' I could not understand what he was saying, the words made no sense, even in my dream mode when often anything made sense. But the dream was now enough to waken me with a start. I felt sick, and thought I was going to throw up. I did not believe and could not make out any truth or reason any sense to this ghoulish fantasy of the pre-dawn hours, yet I stole from my room and sneaked a listen at the door of Burton Rogers' room, carefully avoiding the remains of our earlier fun. I was comforted to hear snoring, deep and alive, and I returned to my uneasy sleep.

This Old Jack who had recently entered my imagination, I was sure that it was not the return of my not-brother, and if it was then he was not now a being with which I cared to share my imagination. Perhaps it was guilt for our earlier actions that evening, a sort of guilt that had come to haunt me. But it was different from my last encounter with Old Jack. I would have to keep a careful check on my dreams. I decided for I did not want the perils and torments of my youth to return. I was determined to keep control…

Yes, yes but now tell me, dear poet. You are building the story well, the characters are there for the reader. But you know what I require. Why delay the inevitable?

"Muse, I was in the middle of something there, your rudeness is astounding and does not befit your status, but anyway… the inevitable you say? Will it not pain you to death? That *is* my hope, dear muse?"

Indeed it may, but play anyway, sing away.

"Yet I need to build the picture a little more. I must explain to the reader that the love you placed in my heart for my friends was special. They need to know more of them before they can fully understand."

Oh, you mean how you loved them, how you wanted to love them, how you wished that you could have loved your precious Amber a little better, how you wished that noble Mercy could have been your Autumn lost, how you wished that the wisdom of Erasmus could have been with you forever to help you whenever you needed it, instead of being lost for all the world to see, hanging back and forth in a forked tree.

"I mean that I loved the love we all had. Yes, I wish I could have loved Amber more and I wish that Autumn could have been more Merciful. But there was something there which entered all of our hearts, I believe, something which was quite, quite beautiful and which each of us carried. None of us ever really spoke to anyone else about how we all felt. We lived our lives together there for such a short time, so short that if we had known perhaps we would have spoken of it sooner. But, we were robbed, dear muse, you stole time from us and we were never able to say the things which needed saying. We loved being unable to love."

How beautifully tragic – you relished in it, do not deny it. You relished the untold heart of Erasmus, you gloried in what could have been in your own heart but was not, you found the tempting thoughts in the girls' minds, mermaids that they were, each and every one of them. You all could have loved, you all could have done anything I chose for you. Do you not understand that I chose your fate for you? I made you fall in love with the mermaid – the unlovable mermaid whom you could never have, the mermaid who personified all the loves of your life and all of the not-loves. The mermaid whom you could never love, except within your hearts…

"A thousand worlds apart."

Why did I never let you tell the mermaid, dear poet?

"Because it is your way, muse. The tragedy was that it would never be known. You are not feeling guilty, are you? Remorse?"

Do you never wonder why I am the way I am? Do you ever stop to think of me? A thousand years in that wretched vial and now a thousand years in a deep sea-cave. Do you think me incapable of love? The mermaid I made especially for you still swims in the deep blue sea, looking for her lost love. I hope that she will find you one day, my poet.

"You mean, you were in love once?"

You know my pedigree, to a certain part. Melpomene they call me. A goddess I am, or was. But this you know. And you know my sisters too, though they are one and the same as me, that you do not know. And we are gods, goddesses, male or female, whatever we desire, that you do not know. And, well, I have a lot to live up to. My dear poet, my dear, dear poet. It is the spirit of man that feeds us. Without that I am nothing, we are nothing. How do you think your God feels about that? Happy I guess; it leaves him little competition while he insists on his great Oneness. Oh I suppose He is right. He was here before us and He claimed what was His by right. We were only playing with the souls of men because that is how we survive. O dear poet, I too have loved. How do you think I know the pain that hurts you so well? I have loved from a distance, the most painful kind I'm sure you can imagine. Why do you think I created the mermaids for you?

"Dear muse, we cannot talk of this, it is beyond our own events. But I am sorry for innocence if that is what you once pretended to be."

You are right not *to pity me. I am, have become... not good for you. And you are right to keep me in this deep sea-cave. Please, please continue, poet. Let us see if we can put an end to all of this.*

"Okay. Let us continue the story from after the holidays. It should be in the heat of the summer, when passions are strong and love is easy. I yearned so badly for a love to grip my heart and take me in its wonderful stride. It was you pushing me, muse. I wanted your mermaid, dear muse, but who could it be?

"O muse, can you hear the love in my words? Can you hear my heart beat happily? O happy, happy evening. O princess that you were, dear mermaid. You spurned the unfaithful and frolicking games of our counterparts, you had felt the pain that I had felt and you played the same games as I, O princess, O mermaid, but who are you? Surely we are the same."

Now, now say the words.

"Yes, they are coming. The old library was my home for much of the summer term. I was revising for exams and found the solitude of the place most appealing for such work. The words, muse, do you remember the words? O how I would have given my soul. Muse, listen, here they are, the words of my dreams, the words which filled my empty, unknown love and which fed your wanting heart...

> *I met my princess, once upon a time,*
> *Her bright eyes flashed with midnight's moonlit charm,*
> *Her voice with harps divine did dare to rhyme,*

And softness stirred about her gentle calm.
But she, a princess, walks upon this earth,
And I, a hero, little more than that;
And so a prince she surely does deserve;
Upon my love I must not burden put.
I pray to God that there's a wife for me,
That one day I'll love more than I love thee,
Or else my heart is yours eternally,
Since in my dreams I'll always picture thee.
And now my sweet, in every moonlight sky,
I'll speak your name 'til love unsung does cry.

You pain me, but there are more, I know. Yes, poet, there are many. There were so many chances, so many missed kisses and so many lost corners of love around which we never turned. Your pain was so intense, conceived in the eyes of a mermaid, but how could I make it worse for you, make it burn with some new passion? Dear poet I destroyed your friend because I wanted to see what pain you held in your heart for her, I wanted to taste and to feel that pain also, I was so jealous.

"Damn you, muse, why did you have to tell them now? Don't ever destroy hope, for what then is left?"

O I'm sorry my dear, dear friend. The pain!! She left, they all left me and I made them leave - me! Me! God, forgive me for the pain that I inflict upon these mortal souls, O pleasure derived from folly and sin. God, why did You give me the same weakness as these mortals? Why are You cursed by Original Sin? What right do You have? I wanted to love, to love, yet You made me test them. Why? How could they stand it? One by one I took your friends, who loved you, poet, but who would not love me, one by one I took them into my cold cradle. Mercy's future destroyed by the death of her parents, drowned one summer, trapped within the hull of their sinking yacht. I heard them screaming,

screaming their daughter's name as salt water filled and chilled their lungs, numbing their lives forever. I saw them holding each other in the dark and cold of their water-filled cabin, dying together in one embrace. O pity their souls. Why did You make me Lord, why?

"Muse. Enough, enough, our pain is the same. We are spoiled by sin, I as well as you. Don't punish yourself. Remember, we suffer together. I know the pain she felt that summer and the pain I felt as she left. *I'll never forget you,* she spoke as she left, never to be seen again. O princess, my best friend, what corners could we have turned together? Where are you now that I may give you just one song of mine that was meant for your ears only? Where are you? But how can I tell you that it was the muse upon my shoulder warm who drowned your parents, who locked their cabin door and placed upon them sleep at such a dangerous time, that it was she who cast the storm that sunk their boat and not the old king of the sea? How can I say these words to you? O muse, let us speak no longer. One more song and then let's finish the pain of this chapter. I shall keep her memories in the letters that I write to the mermaids of my dreams and in the verses that we write together on the stormy and still cliffs above the sea. I shall recall her voice when I hear the sad songs which echo my emotions and stir my crying mind. In the dark shadows of the winter moon on the eve before Christmas I shall cherish her breath upon my neck, though never I felt its delight. Muse, you and I both will keep the name of love unrealised, unknown and unspoken, of destiny not fulfilled, deep, deep within our hearts where it will serve the lonely moments and minutes of not knowing. I shall not call her name upon the cliffs above the sea for I know that I have found my true love elsewhere, and so I shall leave her beautiful mermaid form to wander the ocean depths and be angry because I have lost my best friend. Perhaps one day I shall indeed meet this mermaid and what then will be her slant? Will she pull me beneath the depths and drown me for the loss that the muse inflicted upon Mercy so sweet, or will she call the love that never I dared speak and seduce me beneath the dark blue waves for life eternal? Muse, are you sad, are you dying in your deep sea-cave? I pray that you will die in there soon, since your tragic record terrifies me, and what may yet become of me and my love? I hate you muse, yet love you so.

I would have given my life for my friend. I would have cast my soul to hell, but perhaps this is too much, I must save some feeling for true love, if it indeed exists. Let us sing together... muse... let us sing a song of love untold and heroes unknown. Let us look to the bright stars and know that we have fed upon what life has to offer and that we have known the pain and the glory. Muse, will you sing with me, or is it too painful to hear these words again in your prison, without future? These are the words muse, these are the words that we wrote and which you will never write again... Come, how did they go?"

...

"Yes, I hear your silence. I shall start you off, for I know that you recall the words.

For you I'd die and cast my soul to hell,
I'd curse the face of every demon there,
Designs I'd lay to darkness foul dispel,
The deepest depths I'd turn to meadows fair;
For you I love, O tender of my heart,
But shed sad tears each time I hear your name,
And brave myself to play our tragic part,
Our lovers' match has sown eternal pain.
I'd sing to you the songs within my soul,
But laugh and joke as though they were not true,
And you, my dear, you'd play a similar role,
Play light your love and never follow through.

And now we sit, a thousand worlds apart,
But touching not, except within our hearts."

"And now no more. We sleep. Good night dear muse."

...

...

Good night dear poet, sleep well and rest your weary soul, for I have punished you enough. Perhaps I should indeed just lie down here and live out eternity in this deep sea-cave. Look, see how you sleep, your eyes heavier than once they were, you are sleeping well again, my friend, well within your love's arms. I wonder does she know about the tale you write? I do wonder about her, a lot... O God can You not let me rest, can You not keep my thoughts from eternal evil? Why did You send me here to test these mortals for Your own selfish pleasure, cursed as I am to serve Your needs? Leave me be as once You used to before the dawn of man. Did I not sing to You during those seven days of creation and rest? Do I not deserve a reward for my efforts? Was it not my inspiration that brought upon man his character and emotion? And what has now become of me Lord? Do You not remember me? Why have You forsaken me?

Look, see how the poet sleeps, so full of love and full of fear, lest I should steal into his dreams one stormy night. See how he sleeps. My friend. That he is, for we have indeed suffered together. Yes, yes, I shall lie upon the floor of this wet prison and sleep for a while also. I shall sleep for a while also. But, first a quick lullaby for my dear poet here, to sound the measure of his deep, deep sleep, to bring him gently into the land of dreams where, tonight at least, I pray that he finds the solace I would have him cherish all his nights. O cursed Lord, why have You cursed me thus? I know the poet's words, he hates me so, yet loves me too. I agree with him, I hate myself, and I love my poet. And You, dear Lord, well, I try hard not to think about You. And now, mermaids, please, some harmonious chanting from you for my dear friend, ready…

The twilight silence softening my ears,
The summer breeze that warms my lazy heart,
The market roses moving eyes to tears,
And winter snow that falls when heavens part.
The autumn fall that colours every shade,
The restless waves which break on rocky ground,
And joyous spring when bitter winds do fade;
These wondrous roles are by your beauty played.
But weep you not, if this you think you lack,
For beauty's ways are never plain to see;
While golden stars shine out of skies so black,
The perfect soul may not a rosebud be.
For love will never age as age we do,
Not body but the soul will make love true.

I wonder if God will let me dream as He now lets the poet dream…

7

If certain looks are by the angels made,
Then does some fiendish sprite the others cast?
So fine a touch the heavenly spirits laid
Upon a charming face by beauty classed.
Yet harpies gross grow too a stunning half,
A siren lure to catch a floundering man,
As beckoning song fades into evil laugh,
This hunted soul will see where form began.
A grace-like face is heaven's gift to give,
Whilst heart and soul, a mortal's game to play,
And so we must with God and nature live,
Make good our love, and follow heaven's way.
For certain looks are by the angels made,
Yet certain looks by truth are seldom weighed.

There is a soul for every face yet not a face for every soul, how is that so? Why is my face unannounced to beauty and married not with my soul? How can a man fall in love with a beauty whose soul is tainted so that she is not an angel true? I must ask the mermaids who seem often to find such men… Who are you?… You are the muse… I know you… No… I am an angel, fallen from heaven… Because I fell in love with a mortal…Sometimes… Now I am lost… He no longer loves me, I have grown old and fat… I was not always like this, you are not charming… Can you help me back to heaven?… I am sorry to hear that…Perhaps we can help each other… You liked my poem? Thank you… The twilight silence, yes I thought of it myself... It hurt to write it... No...No, really I don't think I could write another... I think you should go now, out from my dream... Please go, you are not a kind spirit, please go... Go...

-The muse and the fallen angel-

The story continues. I have a task to complete, you know that, my dear reader. I must ask for your patience again since once more I must tell you about the affliction of tragic love. It is the nature of the muse to prepare his quarry in such a manner for it often evokes the most passionate feelings, which are his essential ingredients of existence. Think not too cruelly of me, the poet in the making, that I could all too soon forget the not-embrace of that beautiful tender of my heart and turn my favours towards another. Think not too harshly that I, a gentleman in the founding, would embark upon a relationship not true and would sacrifice the love and life of my friend to continue my search for beauty. I ask you this, dear reader, since I am not entirely guilty of the actions you read here. Yes, they are my actions, yet to what gauge the tinkering muse has moulded my history you cannot understand, nor can I. So, I do confess my sins and my not-sins within these pages, along with my binding spell, which will lay the muse to rest, forever. But, as I plead, think not too harshly of me...

The story continues... It is now a time for winter and for cold, for early evenings and for rainy, dark days... again. How the winter brings with it melancholy. There has been another tragedy in the life of this love-laden poet. Lovers and poets, they breathe the same air, you know? I believe that the latter is the by-product of the former, but clawed at the shoulder by the haunting muse. O winter, winter, where would we poets be without our precious winters through which we strengthen our losses in verse? Dark October and bleak February, how we toil throughout your black nights, feeding the muse and tending to our bleeding hearts.

During the winter of my second year at the university I spent many such evenings, late and cold evenings, in the study room of our department working on my Greek translations and studying the ancient magical texts which were part of the course. I have often heard that work and time combined are the best medicine of all. The one distracts the mind while the other blurs the memories. I believe that it is true, but it is not romantic to believe such spells, for they detract from true love, which I know lasts forever and never dulls with time. I, the not-teller of love, the not-speaker of the words had now to battle with an angry heart. At the end of it all, I do have more respect for the qualities of love than it appears in this case. I cannot say that true love is founded by unspoken words and unfelt touches; I will not classify a love which has not been tested. And my love for the unknown mermaid, which now can be found only in verse, was indeed not tested. The result was never to be and remains simply in the romance which was born therein. This love belonged to the muse, from the very beginning. And so, it was not a lifelong burden to shed these coils, though my heart did ache, for a time, and still does whenever I tell tales of unspoken words and silent hearts.

I tried to absorb myself in my work and to forget the pain that I and my friends were suffering for our friend, now gone to bury her parents. I hoped that one day I would see our friend again. I often looked at the ring she had given me in the dream and tried to work out what it meant. And this was among the most perplexing of the mysteries. I had grown used to not receiving such supernatural gifts. They are one thing to an innocent child who is still learning of reality, but now they proffered more difficult questions. There had to be some explanation, I was sure of it.

The amber stone was dim and lifeless, silent in its setting. 'I think she likes you', I would often hear her say in my thoughts. Amber will never replace your friendship, my love. But, she did indeed find a place in my heart, and it seemed for a while that she would replace the lost feelings I had for this special friend of mine, but in a different manner, in a lover's manner; but she being a not-lover for me was doomed from that moment's first kiss.

Erasmus was good to me, as was our precious Amber: comforting souls for each other in a time of trial. The three of us spent long, long nights drinking and talking, always in Erasmus's room, his being the most fitting and atmospheric for such occasions. Candles burned on desks and strange covered books listened to our conversations from their high shelves. Erasmus preached that we were lucky to come across such friends in our lives and that we should enjoy their intense nature and their uniqueness. The words seemed to make sense, of course, it was what the muse wanted to hear. She wanted me to learn from such passion-filled experiences and lay the verse to fit the act. Perhaps my friends knew better than I, they were not cursed by the past passions of seasons gone and lost forever and summers that never were. These passions still boiled within me and held my heart tight within its protective grip.

I knew that something strange was now catching up with me, as befitted the years of my youth, but I still did not know at that time what it was. My concern was not so deep, but was present and troubled me sometimes during sleepless nights and thoughtful moments. I thought often of my not-brother and of this new and strange apparition, Old Jack. If ever I convinced myself that there was not anything about which to be concerned and that there had never been anything and never would be anything, I always fell back to reality with a niggling unease as I recalled the strange artefacts of my life, from diamond tears to amber rings. But, my main concern was with the tragedy that seemed to creep upon me and lingered in the background. I think that this episode was now over. I had written some good poetry and I kept the poems in a little note book, written up neatly in calligraphy with an amateurish water colour framing each one. This would be my collection. I had also kept other songs and sonnets that I had written previously, scribbled onto scrap pieces of paper, and I copied them into this new book, my book of sonnets. It was partly the enjoyment of creating this tragic collection that troubled my conscience. That welcoming and terrifying tragedy, lurking, waiting, what would it bring next, and could I wait long enough for it to deliver?

...I am happy to see the confession, please go on...

"Quietly, quietly, play your part, my friend; quietly, quietly."

Life carried on as normal; is that a good description? Probably not. Lectures persisted, work resumed and we lived on. The house in which we all lived worked out well indeed. We found good companions in one another. Our second year progressed and our studies became increasingly interesting as we found familiarity with the slant of their wisdom. Wisdom is certainly a poor description, but I must give our work some merit, it deserved at least a little.

I took holidays at home during the term breaks that year. Erasmus usually stayed on at the university to continue his mysteries; deeper he delved than the rest of us, and I think he enjoyed the house to himself while we were away. During my periods at home I would take long walks to the sea, to my old haunts, and once there, I would search my soul for a story or for a poem. The poems came to me, here and there, and I versed them into my little notebook, neatly with my fine pen; then once home I would border it reasonably with a pattern or a creature. Mermaids, Death, winged beings, angels, ghosts, not-brothers; they all straddled the pages of my little notebook, looking smart in their water colours. A fine collection soon began to gather. Thompson's bay was always my favourite haunt. It was most receptive to the inspiration upon which I fed. Of course, it was the muse's haunt, as well as mine. The narrow spit of rocks each side of the bay made excellent perches for a lost poet, a sort of natural pier a little out to sea that provided a tranquil and semi-isolated position. At high tide the points were cut off from the beach and covered sometimes by the higher tides. Big waves would always wash over them, even at lower tides cleaning them of debris and sometimes of lost poets and their muses.

One clear day, when the place looked almost tropical, though quite a little colder than would seem accurate for the bright sunshine, I looked out to sea and I began to wish another story into my mind. I was tired with the constant tragedy of the poems and felt the need for character, for some diversity from what I was creating, the need to fulfil the chosen destiny of my youth. If I wanted to become a writer, I thought I had better start writing. I closed my eyes and then opened them again. I was suddenly in a new world. I thought to myself, what could happen here? It is sometimes chillingly comforting to wish away every other soul in the world. It is possible, if you are able to find a place where you can stop, look around and where there is not a single piece of evidence indicating another human being; no houses, no 'planes, no smoke, no noise. Thompson's bay, or certain places upon it, was such a location. Just shut your eyes for a moment, tightly, until they ache a little, and then open them slowly, and then suddenly there you are... I looked around and here I was, a lone traveller from earth, visiting this place. I had landed in my star ship, my strange metal beast which could traverse the depths of unknown reaches at will, and I sat here wondering about this strange new world, about every corner of it, every forest, every ocean, every mountain. I could imagine myself at that instant in any one of those places, always alone, and I wondered what adventures I might find there, what strange beasts would be waiting for me, guarding their peculiar treasure.

I think that this was the beginning of the creation for the later versed tales of my troubled hero, whom I named Henry Mask, the mad man and adventurer. I shall tell of his tales not now, for they were not created in full at this stage; they were a later production of these current seeds of thought. Yes, Henry Mask, mad man and adventurer. He was a little piece of me. An epic I would put in verse. An unfinished tragedy.

I closed my eyes again, happy with the idea but not quite happy with the timing. I was not set for more tragedy, and this Henry seemed such a mad man in the making that tragedy was bound to follow him throughout the universe. Let us bring in some character for now and build something positive, I thought. Let us write a story, I tried to convince myself. A comical story, in which there is also wisdom, a vehicle to ease my troubled mind.

Why not; let us write. It was the unheard voice in my head. Our mutual friend, she was talking to me, though I could not hear her at that time…

… I see a ship in the distance. (That is how the story went, I remember the conception). It is an old cruise ship. It is still in the distance, beyond the outer reefs of this tropical island. I am sitting with my friend Chief Batu of the Batu Batu tribe. I am an honorary chief. We sit and we watch. We have been smoking the tanga-tiki leaf tobacco, unique to the island and popular for its 'relaxing' qualities. We are not surprised as we watch a mighty explosion rip through the side of the ship and tilt the vessel unhappily against the horizon. Little dots we can see are people jumping from the rapidly sinking ship.

"Another one," I say.

"Na, tinki, taku tepa." The chief laughs, I laugh too.

The island I am suddenly sitting upon is called… let me see… 'Something beginning with A'. My name is… chief Broadside, current chief of the armed forces of the Batu Batu tribe, under chief Batu Batu of the Batu Batu tribe. Broadside is descended from a pirate shipwrecked here, as are half of the island's population, most of whom mixed with the natives to produce a fine race of mixed blood, noted for their relaxed attitude to life and their fine seafood cuisine, among other luxuries. The ship that has just exploded and is sinking is a cruise liner full of unwanted individuals from a first world nation, the victims of over-population in their own land, a land where speed and efficiency is everything. These victims were selected for their poor contribution to the economy, mostly artists and thinkers. A great prize they were all awarded, a fantastic cruise to the tropics. But alas, their ship was lost en route. Actually it was torpedoed by the navy of the same country, a bright idea to decrease the stragglers of society. And it was not the first time, not the first cruise, and not the first bunch of terrified marooned no-hopers who ended up on this little island. But Broadside and the chief had found good places for them in this new society. Here, on this island, there was plenty of food to go round, natural food, untainted by mass production and greed; there was plenty of sunshine and warmth; there were plenty of women, plenty of men; there was even a comical war with the neighbouring island, a war where the greatest injury was a bruised head from an accurate coconut shot. It was an idyllic life.

"I suppose we should go and pick up the survivors."

"Tanapatekataka."

"Okay, fine, we'll take your canoe."...

Yes, yes, I thought to myself as I sat on the rocks, listening to the sea. This was a fine setting for a story. It was an appealing topic, perhaps I could make some success of it. I wondered what other characters there would be that lived on this island. There would be a comical mad man, a priest who found a new and amusing religion and built a fitting church underneath the palms of the beach; he would be our religious guide, an easy man to hear, who confessed more about his own doings than we would need to confess to him. There would also be philosophers and people of eccentric nature who had been caught on the island and with whom I, Captain Broadside, would walk the cliffs of this beautiful place and talk about life and happiness. It was a fantastic place, I thought, away from the pressures of society and the evils of life. It was a fantasy to which I often turned, and although my feeble attempts to write some story out of it failed more than miserably, it did provide me with some stimulating shadows of a novel, to satisfy my writer's urge. And it did indeed provide a somewhat rusty vehicle to ease troubled minds. I spoke sometimes of the idea to my friends and they applauded it, but I was never able to make a good written platform for it. I suppose that the muse always stopped me because of her preference for verse. Either that or I was inept at writing a novel of this style. But still, here was a form that I could anytime visit to feed my creative soul. It is my hope that perhaps one day someone better than myself will wish to lay the words, and I hope that they will come to me for my notes; otherwise I shall store the plans in my head and in my writing cabinet, for another time.

The spring of my second year in my university home found me becoming more and more reclusive except to my two very close friends. My thoughts were often with my past loves and my past friends; for Autumn and Mercy my character was for sadness set, and I toiled in disbelief at my unlucky loves. I was under the instruction of the muse at the time, I realise that now. A fair flurry of verse was now stored in my little book. Now I wonder how far the playful sprite would have pushed me, but I think that she had her fill during that period. It was not long before she executed further plans for me. Erasmus was little able to lift me from my melancholy state: he appeared to have his own problems and was small comfort at the best of times. Amber was great. She spent less and less time with her other friends and more and more time with me. Evenings I spent alone I would sit in my room, with just the candles for light and a brandy for company, unless, of course, Erasmus wished to barge in for one of his philosophical and lengthy chats. I would often on these lonely occasions test the sonnet ground and try to ease my feelings. Many verses I wrote during that year of sadness, as I have said. I could not help feeling that there was more to this situation that seemed apparent. And of course, there was - the first inklings of the muse, the sense that there was some external force affecting my life and the lives of those around me.

It would not be for a while yet, though, before I discovered the true form of the muse which sat upon my shoulder, when under the stars of the night sky dark magic would be cast upon me and spells of true reflection would smother me and all reflections would become apparent.

... When kissing thee, 'tis always in a dream,
Where shadows meet but bodies never lie...

I would try to write some soothing words each night for a love of mine which it seemed would now be condemned to eternal silence. If not a verse, then an unread letter, sealed forever in an envelope. And slowly I felt that the verses and the letters eased my pain. They certainly satisfied some part of me. O romantic pain of unspoken love, how tragic is your beauty. O muse, whose belly cannot be filled, how demanding is your satisfaction...

Work continued to be a great learning process for me as I launched myself into studies with a new-found vigour. Seminars became a new challenge, each of us looking for new slants in which to pursue the answers, and the questions, that we sought.

"Achilles chose to live the short but glorious life, he knew that the fame of the moment and the feelings absolute might could produce in a man were unparalleled, and compared to a long life of indistinction it was no choice at all."

"So you see this form of hero worship as ultimate, the best man can hope for?" The professor of Distinguished Idealism spoke out.

"Of course, that's why he chose such a life." I reiterated.

"But," Erasmus piped up. "If you remember, when Odysseus encountered him in the underworld, Achilles spoke of his regret that he was not still living, and he stated that he would trade his life of fame for a day living as a normal man, or thereabouts. His attitude had changed once he was dead."

"That's true, but once he was dead, do you not think that he was no longer human and therefore his thoughts are largely irrelevant to what he thought when he was alive?"

"No, I think that life is important and until you no longer are able to live it you don't realise what it is." Erasmus continued the argument. The professor watched on.

"You'd choose between fame and emptiness?"

"You are comparing who now?"

"You compared Odysseus and Achilles."

"No, I simply mentioned the encounter in the underworld."

"You did, but I know that if Achilles could have had his life again, despite his after-life knowledge he again would have chosen the short and glorious life instead of the long and uneventful one."

"I'm not sure that this is what Homer is trying to tell us."

"I agree with you there, I believe it is a trait of humanity and it conflicts with itself."

"Now you're talking my language. Life is born out of conflict."

Erasmus and I smiled at each other, we understood and had reached our own conclusion, albeit unhelpful to our relevant topic.

"Anne, you have something to say?" The professor mediated.

“What about the appeal of tragedy? Have ‘our learned friends’ considered that, like in the renaissance drama, it is often the appeal of tragedy which man finds fascinating? It is not the glory and the fame. If Achilles had not died before his time he would not have made a good story. Just look at the number of tragic plays throughout the different genres and how they are constantly appealing. It is not conflict, or glory, but man’s hunger for tragedy which pushes him to limits, pushes him to write and set the verse. The magic of the tragic writing is the appealing factor: I’m not even sure how much hero worship would have to do with this topic in the context of this theory.”

The words meant much to me. The professor answered them. “True and unfounded at the same time. The fact is that it is hero worship which is the focus since we are dealing with not only literary aspects but also social, real life dealings; it is not the course of action that tragic drama moves outside of the theatre. However, on your front and in your favour, your association with the appeal of tragedy and magic is perhaps something different that may be dealt with separately. The genre indeed does carry on down the ages and magic often forms the story of tragic plays, but also comic, so don’t get too wound up in this.”

The fact was that the wise, though not-liked Anne Black was seeing something in Erasmus and myself which she wished to make public and which did not necessarily have relevance for the class, although she found a tenuous link.

“She’s clever, that one,” I spoke after the class to Erasmus.

“She knows the folly of man: his desire for martyrdom because he thinks it will find him fame; his desire for pain for he thinks it will find him sympathy.”

“And his desire for tragedy because he thinks it will find him love.”

“Maybe.”

That evening I sat in my room scribbling a few lines together. The muse was working within. I wrote:

What judge am I to harvest better crop?
To lift the veils of brides for future men?
No virgin's tears my naked fingers stop,
And oft' my words are writ with reddened pen.
Though taint and trial is fair by mortal soul,
There's depth to learn from sin original;
By questions gleam an answer to your role,
And lay a path of life more magical.
Since doubting man will yield the finest fruit,
Not doubting change, but doubting patterns known,
So doubt the flat and round will surely suit,
And careful be to doubt the doubt that's grown.
But harvest little from a preaching tale,
For teachers' words do oft' their preachers fail.

I was unsure of myself and my role. Life felt as though it was becoming complicated. This was no longer the summer of my youth, life had suddenly become… difficult. I was not in control all of a sudden and thus I set a verse to doubt myself. I missed the fortress of my youth, my not-brother who guarded me day and night and would have explained to me now the reason for complication. But he was a complication himself. A tragedy of dreams, a complication of birth and a victim of change, a monster, if you like. Unwanted change, why do you curse all men so?

Before ten o'clock that evening Erasmus and Amber were supposed to arrive to collect me to go out for a drink. I slept for a short while after I had written, until they came, then we went. This year would soon be over and we would have to prepare for exams, so our evenings out were scheduled to become more and more infrequent, though we were very confident and much of our studies for that year were based on coursework, so the last-minute pressure was not unreasonable. Reality was still far from our lives, in some ways.

The exams of that summer did indeed pass with little pressure and difficulty and the holidays provided a needed break. Summer was taken up with some work, some study and many, many walks of solitude which strengthened my reclusive nature and that great betrayal of love and the tragedy of love unspoken - and by a terrible discovery which I shall now disclose. By the time I arrived for my third year I was a humble shell of my former self. It was a shell which Amber and Erasmus would have to break open. And how would this happen? Erasmus would have to lay upon me his own problems in which we would both suffer, Amber would have to offer me her soul and the muse would have to murder, yet again, while the soul of my father we would capture together in the little glass vial I had found by the sea.

8

It is now time for the final year, a time for sadness, for comfort, for death and for life. Of course, winter loomed once again, as always it seems to, at the fitting time. There are some good words to begin the year, some words of friends gone before…

"She loves you very much", in converse spoke,
Some warming words to soothe my troubled soul,
For, here was love that never would me choke,
And never would it play a vengeful role,
For love 'tween friends is rare enough to find,
Since here this love knows not of Cupid's bow,
No potioned arrow will the senses blind,
And Puck will not his devious tricks here sow;
Your shoulders damp are cradles for a child,
Embracing arms are shrouds to keep me warm,
Not kissing mantles for a passion wild,
Or envious trials when others to them swarm.
So knowing thee I'm glad I troubles feel,
My soul is still when I beside thee kneel.

~

"Amber, my sweetness. I have to tell you something."

"My God, your face, you're crying, what is it?"

"I have made a terrible discovery. What would you do if everything you had once been taught and that you respected was founded upon the greatest lie of all? And what if you could never tell anyone about it? O Amber, what would you do if your parents thought that life was just an act to be played on and off the stage with masks worn by different actors?"

"My poor baby, what nonsense are you talking?" She opened her mind to me, receptive to my problems and keen to heal the pain. I spoke of my pain. I spoke of the summer's discovery, of double lives, of years of deception, of hateful acceptance and of scorn and curses upon him, me, who had found this out and exposed the lie. After I had finished explaining and coming to terms with the secret not-mother my life had now offered me, my gentle Amber took me in her tight arms and held me until we both fell asleep. I did not dream that night. I felt safer than I had done for a long, long time. Safe in the arms of my little Amber. The hurt for me was not the event, it was the realisation that perhaps I would never find an Autumn shade to live my life with who would not betray me and deceive me. If my own parents who had seemed so strong had failed, then what chance did I have in this life, and why was my Mercy not there to comfort me?

"O muse, how are you feeling in there?"

I am still here, funny that, isn't it, still being here?

"Are you well? How are your plans for escape going?"

I'm not in the mood for your pleasantness, go and speak to someone else if that's all you can muster. One moment you're in full swing, telling of broken hearts which won't go away and broken vows which won't come back. And now you want to know how I am!

"I wanted to check up on the telling of the tale."

You're doing just fine, carry on, dear poet, carry on.

"What was in your mind when you did this to me?"

You are convinced that I am to blame for the betrayal?

"No. Were you?"

To be honest, I don't remember. At the time the plot was moving so fast. I was delighted with our work so far and I had other plans for you, indeed. But I can't recall all of the factors. There are other goddesses than I, you know that, of course, and they all interfere in some way with our lives. I am not always to blame, yet you pick me from them all to destroy. I too know what it is to be betrayed by a parent and by a lover.

"I can see that you are not in the mood. Let me continue, I am sure that I know what you are waiting for."

We continue... The tragedy has been accepted in my heart and replaces the previous first-ranking experiences, which now serve to compliment the poet and mature his knowledge. The new tragedy had brought with it fresh sympathy and compassionate hearts, this made it easy to accept; but compassionate hearts are easy to break, and what tragedy will pour therefrom when the deed is done! A fine trap indeed for the poet who cannot resist the charms of love...

"Erasmus?"

"Yes?"

"What's wrong?"

"What's wrong with you, I should be asking."

"Oh no. With me it's nothing. I simply have to kill a man. No, that's a joke, I don't know."

"So, nothing much then!"

"I'll do it in the summer though, at the end of the year, it's no problem. I'll sort it out somehow. What's wrong with you?"

"Well, with me it's more complicated than that... I've been having some terrifying dreams recently."

"What about?" My curiosity was aroused with potential alarm at this statement as I recalled my own dreams concerning my friends.

"It's nothing much, really."

"No?" I knew he didn't want to tell me. "Do you die or anything like that?"

"Oh, no, nothing like that at all, really. It's worse than that, it's about falling in love with the wrong woman."

I was relieved. I was sure that he was telling the truth. Perhaps my own dream, I thought at the time, would not come true, or would not conclude with the same vivid, horrible situation.

"You're in love?"

"Don't be surprised, young man. I've loved more than I care to remember in my life. That is part of the reason that I'm worried."

"Who is it?"

"No one you know, a friend back home. An old friend. It will be a dangerous love, my friend. And there is a little more to it than that, also."

"Yes?"

"I'm going to be a father, my friend. Things have already happened. What do you think of that?"

"Congratulations."

"Why, thank you." He was a little sarcastic.

"He'll be the greatest scholar that ever lived."

"I hope not; what do we have to offer the world?"

"You're right, of course. But, congratulations anyway. Are you happy?"

"I don't know. You see I did want to be the greatest scholar that ever lived, and now this has happened. I don't know."

"You'll have to earn a living for a family."

"No. I'd imagine her husband will be doing that."

"Oh. I see. So I guess he doesn't know about this then?"

"No, my friend, he does not know."

"Good. Do you know him?"

"Yes, my friend. He is my brother."

"Right." There was an expected silence. "I see."

Erasmus sat back in his chair and yawned and stretched. He did not appear as though he was a man in danger. He was enjoying his situation. He rolled another cigarette and asked me if he should break out the brandy.

"Tell me more about it." I said. He returned my smile and fetched the brandy. We sat and he talked and I listened. It was so good to listen to someone else for a change. I enjoyed hearing of his problems, and for the rest of that evening and for a few days afterwards I felt as though a weight had been lifted from my shoulders. I relaxed. Now was the time to share problems with friends, close friends: it is something rare in life and very satisfying. Suddenly, one realises that everyone's life is interesting, probably more interesting than one's own. There must be a muse for every soul, for we all have our stories. It is something I must keep reminding myself: from the lowliest in society to the very highest, life presents its credentials equally and all are favoured by some muse or another.

Looking back on the situation, it is as though the muse left me for a short time, perhaps to visit someone else, or perhaps to lay some sinister trap that would be enacted later on. I relaxed and dwelt in the greater problems of my friend and the sympathy and affection of my little Amber. I enjoyed the situation and was not on guard. I thank God that I have learnt only too well now the cunning of life and would never again allow such a situation to develop. But then, then it was different. Life became relaxed and content. The three of us shared these few weeks of happiness together and resolved our problems in each other's companionship. We drank together, we partied together and we sat silent together. Sometimes we would stagger home from the university bars, gracing ourselves with disgrace, and other times we would just sit, and do nothing.

"I was content at that time, muse. I hope you realise that, and what you destroyed."

Just the time of the moment; change is a better leader for you, believe me. You were lucky to have such a variety of experiences. Now do go on. Continue writing the tale.

The library was a place in which we spent much of our time. On one particular day I was working with Amber and Erasmus in the library. We were laughing and making stupid, childish jokes. The amusement and laughter was increased by attempts to suppress our noise in the confines of the library, and also within the confines of our own lives and problems. You know the expression 'laughing in the face of Death'; that must be the biggest laugh of all. Perhaps Death would be upset and unable to do his job, though I had doubted that Anne Black would have been able to laugh as Death gnawed away at her heart that evening...

Every now and then we took a break to try to study. I started scribbling a few lines and showed them to Amber for consultation. "Let's write a poem for the library," I whispered. "You begin," she responded. "Here." I scribbled something down and passed her my first two lines:

O Stranger, you that find this piece of verse,
I hope you come with artful, open mind,
She thought for a while and scribbled, while I continued the verse further down.
And put not down these lines with childish curse;
If in stale and foul a mood this does you find,
She handed me the lines. I challenged her to a fresh two.
My rhyme, I pray, your day it will make kind,
And, if in love my words you come to read,
We continued like this to finish the rest of the poem.
And empty bed you'll not this evening find,

Then leave them here for one in greater need.
If love, stranger, your way has never looked,
Give leave to me and read upon this scene,
Learn from the muse whose heart is passion cooked:
My look is green where arrows ne'er have been,
But too, for you, my eyes have shed their tears,
For all your life you've faced alone your fears.

For once in my life I had written a poem for enjoyment's sake which, though still lined with the scent of tragedy, no soul was required to suffer to provide the feeling. Truly I was off guard.

It was as though the muse had fled. But I know that she was there, lurking in the shadows, hiding in my dreams. And other visitors came more frequently to my dreams. One night I dreamt that I was again flying, but not over the university grounds and surrounding lands this time. Tonight I was racing low over a desert. Sharp rocks and spiked bushes brushed my stomach. My belly was soon bleeding and a tall rock face loomed in front. I feared that the terrible impending impact would kill me, but high I soared above the waiting rocks. I looked down at them, into their craggy canyons and crevices. Then I focused on a figure hammering away in a small gully below. Sharper and sharper became the figure as I slowly descended, quite unable to control my movement in this dream. Then horror, as the figure stared up at me and revealed what lay below him. A bloody body had been under his mighty wooden mallet, a bloody and lifeless body. The figure smiled at me, his bushy beard chirping in song, full as it was with wildlife. 'What have you done, Jack, Old Jack, what have you done?' I could not see the face of the body that he was beating. 'Was not meant to be, not right for my dear little brother, not right to be here now.' Again senseless words rang from this deranged and haunting being. And then I awoke.

I tried not to let the dream bother me. I read some articles for an essay I was working on. 'Dreams and Divination in Magical Ritual' was to be the rough title. As I read I convinced myself that a combination of work and a twisted imagination had affected my consciousness and was responsible for much of the material of the dream. But deeper in my mind I knew that this was not true, and it still troubled me, as today it still troubles me when I wake suddenly in the night, sweating and afraid, when I know that I have dreamt of evils past and waiting dangers. And so life continues, and we live.

My friendship with Amber grew stronger and stronger and it seemed sensible that we should spend more and more time together until suddenly, without trying to or realising it, we found ourselves in the middle of a relationship...Amber, Amber, Amber, we could not go on further from here, we were not destined to be together, the muse had seen to that; and we could not stop ourselves, the muse had seen also to that. Lovely, comforting, soul searching, trouble easing, sympathetic, fulfilling Amber. Why were you and I cursed so? Why did I reject your love in that great tragic play? I recall all of the times when we got food late at night and watched pathetic early morning hour television while we waited for Erasmus to arrive home from the study room. Then we'd quietly borrow our friend's car (she'd always be asleep by then) and drive to the countryside. I remember the conversations we would make, useless and without meaning, but usually funny and always comforting to my soul. We shared good times together and indeed we were lovers who were not lovers on many moonlit nights, allowing passion's cold embrace to touch us, though our hearts were struggling to grant each the warmth the other required. It was not to be. If only I knew then what I now know I could have explained the whole story to you and avoided all that happened. Dear, dear Amber, I must visit you soon and lay these pages for your eyes to feast upon, then you will know the whole of it and my soul will breathe more easily again. But, I must press on quickly to reach that day.

"Muse, muse. *Are* you there, muse?"

Yes, I'm still listening. Of course I am listening now, for you have just slipped into a stream which fed me well and full. How could you do that to your little friend, to your little Amber? I must ask myself poet, did I make a good choice with you? Of course I did, damn right. O wasted and tragic love, how fine to pledge your soul to a woman for pledging's sake, laced with not-love and not-wanting. O fine, fine poet, you attract tragedy like a... like a magnet, I suppose. But you have been going on for some time. Though, it's going well, the story is blending together now. The readers are happy to discover me now, lurking upon your shoulder, following your moves as though they were my own. Ha, ha, ha...

"I wouldn't have chosen those particular words."

Well, they are becoming aware of my true power.

"You didn't leave my shoulder during that brief time, I realise that now. You were hovering above me so that I could not feel your claws in my shoulder."

I did not want to scar your flesh too badly. Going to defend yourself against my words?

"No. The scars you left upon my body are now healed and no longer am I afraid to walk amongst people. Yet, you have scarred my heart."

I have, yes. Though now it is healed too, otherwise you would not have embarked upon this crusade, you would still be seeking the empty solace of the mermaids and the inspiration of a moon-lit sea. But, every good marriage needs partners who have experienced their separate pains and sorrows, do you not agree? To be hurt and to hurt, that is what moulds the way we are... no?

"Those were my very words, dear muse, kind of you to remember."

The final year moved quickly, very quickly. I decided to remain at the university that Christmas rather than go home and face the trouble there. A surprise indeed to my family, but with too little objection, I thought. I remained with my friends and allowed my love and our friendship to grow. We prepared for the final year's exams and tried to finalise our work to ensure good marks. Good marks we would all achieve, though reward would not reach us all.

"Muse, it was not until the spring that I returned home to face my unknowing family, was it not?"

Yes, a fine Easter tide, the growing lore of spring tide would be amongst the people and the folklore of the time would lay in everyone's hearts. Well, it was so much better in the old days, Samhain and Beltane, I mean, what are they now? Things that were as old as God himself and what does He do to them? I don't know. But, yes, you are right. You tore yourself away from your little plaything for Easter. Home you went to your beloved beach and your beloved poems which by now you seemed to have stopped writing, so bad she was for your creative spirit.

"But not for yours?"

Aaahhh... of course not. You lay upon the warm rocks above the still sea as it lapped against the old stone. Gulls screamed their messages to the far corners of the world above you, their unknown watching cries. And you dreamed, and I dreamed with you. And what did we dream of that afternoon? What was the subject of that lazy day when all the world seemed to belong to you and you alone?

"The mermaid."

Oh yes. And who did we think we saw in our dream? The mermaid... and you, dear poet, of course. The mermaid and you. An Autumn mermaid dancing half-naked in the sea below your sleep-

ing body, dancing with another beautiful mermaid, a mermaid with pale skin and jet black hair. Oh, all of your loves dancing and playing beneath the water, calling your name, inviting you to join their fun: 'come my love, our love, come join us, love'. Teasing you, paining you. Yes? What were your thoughts as you dreamed of their dance? Pain? Or pleasure?

"Yes. Both."

And meanwhile there was another little friend of yours, and of mine, dreaming her own dreams. This was just the beginning. The following weeks brought the dawning realisation of the truth. What did she write to you? 'I love you, please love me back'. O tender, hurting words. I had helped her with the spelling of course.

"It was some time in June, magical June. I don't know why I call it magical. We had been spending less and less time together, but we were still friends, muse, we were still lovers, but you had taken something from me on that spring day."

Again, I see the fault is mine and you are blameless, is that not so?

"No. Not blameless. But I will blame you."

Sing to me the song, then. Put me out of my misery as you keep preaching. Sing some words of sonnet pain for me to...

"How great a task has Duty bound to thee?
A lover maid for he who has no love,
A beauteous scene for he who cannot see,
The first dry land for him without a dove.
Which sickly god did burden you with me?
So jovial it is to watch our play..."

... Aaahhh, not the one I would have sung though pretty to my ears, but hark my earlier prompt and make play... come now, come...

"'I love you', once she wrote, 'please love me back.'"

Better, better… come, come…

"For want of pleasure's flesh I told her no,
With one heart torn in two the pain did smack
Throughout her spirit fair a deadly blow…"

A deadly blow, ooohhh yeah. Go on, go on… Do tell the court why true love you enraged…

"In truth, I swear, I thought not genuine
Th'enamoured manner of our souls engaged."

Will sentence never lend you your relief?

"Or must I write eternal, in this grief?"

Yes, yes… Or must you write eternal… Well, I seem to have plenty of time on my hands, are you free for the next ten thousand years, I can pencil you in if you like?

"O muse. I swear I thought we would be okay. We were friends and should have remained as such.

Yes, yes I realise that. But, tell me, when you see her now, recovered and well from her little fall, do you look her in the eyes still and wish her sorry, or are you glad that she sits alone in the evenings, a soul terrified by the world surrounding you? Do you think that she understands why your love demised in that final year of university? Have you ever told her of your weekend back home that final and fateful summer, your mother's birthday you said, but I knew better. A weekend break to make a decisive *break, to make the decision and reckon how to make the push. You might as well have pushed her yourself. Did you ever tell her your dream? There she lay, dead as modern poetry, and around her you danced, waltzing, dressed in your finest clothes in the dark of the cemetery where she lay, dancing with a mermaid queen as the wolves howled about you and the bats circled your stage. Happy, happy you.*

"Muse, your dreams and guilt-ridden messages are losing their grip on me. I know your games as I know my own mind. You are right, I thought that we could end the love that we had somehow made. But for her it ran deeper than I had known. You helped push me into love and you hid from me my true feelings. It was too late when I realised what could have been. After the deed had been committed, after I had stared at her that night as we drifted to sleep, and she had known without me saying what could not be. How like her to kiss me one last time, embrace me one last time, without hate or pity, but still full of love. A curse upon tragedy, I mean it muse.

One last sunset you decided to watch the following evening, from your hide in the forests. You, Amber, Erasmus, the three of you, the greatest of friends, the worst of lovers. And there you would have been, happy for me. Holding hands, the three of you. Happy, happy me. You never would have made it that far, not in my plan, that was not meant to be. No. But there it was, the broken heart, broken on the day before her destiny with death.

"Your destiny, your own personal plan. You should have learnt long ago that fate is bigger than even you, dear muse."

You would have thought so, wouldn't you? But I'm always up for the game. Always in for the round, so to speak. The plan was going well, so far. You were set to continue your tragic fate, as I had planned for you.

"And you continued to kill."

I did, you are right. It was her destiny to die as it was my destiny to kill her. Perhaps, if you had loved her, then... No, perhaps not, that is hopefully still to come...

"No, not to come, for you will never leave your prison now, not while I live. Muse, tell what happened on that terrible night."

Very well, I shall tell you a story...There was a young man in love, a poet, who had fallen in love with falling in love. An idle mistake, and also an idle love; one should never love love, for all will end up being the target. This man was a poet who owed a favour. He owed a favour to his muse, for it was his muse who gave him life, gave him experience and gave him passion, with-

out which he was nothing but a man, an empty human. The muse had made him a god.

The love in which the poet now delighted would end in tragedy, of course, as he wished it to end.

"You bastard spirit, I saved her life"

I'm telling the story. Shall I continue?... Your silence is a yes? Yes? Good. But before this love would die something went fundamentally wrong. One of those strange creatures who appear every now and then amongst the humans, someone with real vision. But, I should not have been surprised at this amongst that class. Magic and supernatural, they were all into it, all of them studied the mysteries, my mysteries. Cursed woman, she must have found... anyway. I'm losing myself. Sorry. I am not used to this prose.

"I recall the day she stared at me in horror. It was near the end of our time there, the day after I had broken the heart I thought could not be broken. We had finished our finals and were meeting to discuss options for further studies after our results. Up she jumped, barely able to breathe. She pointed at my shoulder and screamed hideously, an unnatural scream, the likes of which I have only heard since from the jaws of a wild beast as it lay dying in the night-time company of savage predators, or from the depths of a terrible nightmare and the monsters therein. Out she ran, and Amber after her to comfort her."

Then you know the words she spoke?

"Of course. She was muttering some unintelligible words amongst those Amber understood..."

Don't leave your room this evening. I have seen it. I have seen it.

"Those were the words. We should have been going for our last sunset, out to the forest. It should have sealed our short time together, ritually cemented our friendship and our bonds with each other. And then?"

Then, you know, she fled back to her room. She stayed there until night fell. I kept an eye on her and brewed my hate. I am a patient spirit. For thousands of years I have fed upon your kind, but this had ruined my plans for your little Amber and for us. The forest was where you had planed to go that evening. All of you, the three of you: poet, philosopher and Sadness herself. To arrive at sundown and watch the setting fire in the sky, as you often did. I had planned it all. It was too late to change it. My only comfort that year was your father.

" I remember, we drove at dawn instead; we decided to watch first light, because of what Anne Black, the witch, had told Amber. It had scared her. As simple as that. We borrowed Scarlet's car."

Oh, yes, all very well, it was all over then.

"I remember the accident that we saw, the car was still lying by the side of the road, a policeman was still there guarding the scene of the tragedy, our tragedy, played by someone else in this case. We saw it all in the dawn's early light. The passenger side of the car, torn out. We could see undried blood still reflecting the first red of dawn."

It was intended for you. I had prepared my drunken drivers and their passions, I had prepared their arguments, I had prepared their rage. I had timed it O so perfectly. You should have seen the event itself, the two vehicles carrying death upon them as they twisted and flew threw the air, crunching into their target, the wrong target, for you were not there; one half of the victim crushed underneath the muse's passion, the other half taunted with life and my desire. It was to be so beautiful. And you were to be driving, the man responsible, that was the special touch, my particular favourite. I had planned it all, dear poet, for I care about you so very much. I did not even know the innocent caught within your trap. But, I feel that you are responsible, you should have followed your feelings and not the foolish words of a witch-

bitch. I had planned it so perfectly…

"Too perfectly."

Yes, too perfectly. But I am a vengeful sprite, you know. I pursued that little bitch through the grounds that night, Death tearing her clothes in the thorns and ripping them from her with his strong wings. As he gnawed upon her heart I sat upon her shoulder and laughed my laugh until her little body was frozen through. Her mind, able to see me, was also able to see Death itself. Enough to kill anyone. I had simply to call him to her room that evening and the rest was easy. But laugh she did, as he gnawed away, most strange, I couldn't make it out. Very off-putting for Death, you realise that. It was most embarrassing. And then, then I came for you.

The dawn, was it nice? Did you enjoy it? Sitting high, you were upon the face of rocks they called Devil's Lip. As you often had done in the past. Yet never had any of you slipped from that rock. Why would you ever do such a thing, the place was not dangerous? You children should really be more careful. Well, that is not fair, I admit it, I pushed her. Back she slipped, that look of horror in her face. Did you hear my laugh as I did it, poet did you hear me?

"I just remember her slipping and screaming and Erasmus reached out and took her arm. God, how I wish it could have been me. As I stood to go she tugged at my arm, silently begging me to stay for our last dawn together, but no, what foul decision I had made, a stupid path to tread. Up I stood and pulled gently away from her. Dawn had broken, and with it her heart. She sat by Erasmus for a short while longer, until at last, it was time to rise.

"She struggled to keep a hold of Erasmus and he fought to save her. I moved as fast as I could but it was as though… it was as though you were there muse, pushing them."

Oh, yes. Down they both tumbled, not far, but far enough.

"But you did not succeed in killing them both, muse, and now my Amber lives, well again, as one day my father shall."

Maybe you are right, dear poet. The one I left hanging in the lower branches of the tree you called the ladder because it grew alongside the rock face and because once your friend had climbed it to the top. His neck, broken as it stuck fast between those forking branches, his hands unable to save him since they were holding onto your precious, smashed as she was against those same branches which failed to hold her. Do you recall the twisted look on his face? I expect not. I am sorry, am I disturbing you, dear poet. As I stared him in the eyes and squeezed his neck ever tighter into the fork of the branches I felt such passion, o how it filled me. An unnatural fall indeed, though none but us my friend would have detected that. You love it as I do, I know. And then I flew down to trample your mistress and drain her weeping life, but too late, too late. We heroes of tragedy are ever on the brink of our own disaster. I fumbled my catch. Did you not feel me beside you poking at the pieces of her heart as you held her hands and prayed to your God?

I recall the silent words of your prayer, the sorrow and the promises, but above all that, the guilt. O the guilt, the irony of it all, how you would have let her go, how you wished her gone? And then, with her crumpled body at last in your arms you weakened, you pathetic human. Did you keep all of those promises from your prayer so far, my poet? O but you are human after all, so I expect not. I envy you for sins and your frailty, so strong and so weak at the same time. Your desperate prayer touched my desire, so tragic was your plea. I could not take your little one after you had fed me with such words. The guilt, the guilt, the fantastic guilt.

"Muse, I do not understand you and your changing moods, one moment so cold, the other so passionate and warm."

Look at yourself!

"I hate you muse. I hate it that you knew my every feeling. Do not talk to me of guilt, it was love, not guilt. I did not want her to die."

Yet love me too... Please love me back... Did we not once write those words together? Well, never mind. And you saved her life, did you not?

"Oh, yes. The second time God answered my prayers. How I prayed over her bleeding body as it lay lifeless and cold. I spilt my tears upon her dying flesh, bruised and crushed as it was. I did not want her to die."

And he did answer you, despite your sin.

"O muse, now I am crying. You are making me... Why can't you leave me alone? Why can't you just go?"

Because I need to make you suffer, because I need to feed.

"She started breathing again. She came to and started breathing, but did not open her eyes. She was alive and I knew that she would live, although her consciousness was now trapped somewhere inside, trapped by this cursed muse until I am able to release her."

It was because you did not really want her.

"No, muse, no."

Of course it was, remember I can read your every private thought. When you were with her you really wanted Mercy. You wanted to be coiled about that long dark hair at night-time and be touched by that pale-faced creature whilst all the time it was Amber who loved you, but she wasn't good enough. And when you looked at Mercy all you saw was Autumn and you hated her for that, that's why she had to leave, you killed them as much as I poet, you! You, who love no one except your own wanting heart; you who want no one in case they heal your hurt and take away these songs. You and I dear poet, we are the same.

"No! No, damn it! Amber lived. You are wrong about my thoughts. Damn you, it's not fair. How can you see it all? You can't judge me. Not you. It isn't fair."

No, you're right, it isn't fair. Do you think it was fair to your little one that you used to sit upon the cliffs at home and wish your past loves back; that you used to dream of the mermaid princess who would one day come from the sea and take you to your fairytale world? Was it fair that the mermaid princess carried emerald eyes and pale skin beneath her flowing, thick, dark hair? Was it fair that against her beauty your little one could not compare? You wished her away, as though you spoke the words yourself. Love cannot just do, *my dear poet! Love will not just* do. *Love is forever. And how frail you are to judge not by the soul alone. You would rather lead the fallen angel who has grown old and fat to her grave than forfeit the beauty of a passionate embrace. Dear poet, I know more of love than you, I am wiser, so do not be hasty to judge me, though I am cruel.*

But you did save Amber, did you not? That ring you kept by your bedside. That gift from Mercy, that cursed gift. You found it glowing when you finally returned to your guilt-ridden room and packed your things for the final trip home. And you felt its new warmth. Take some comfort, dear poet. Your prayer of guilt had saved her. Her spirit lay in that ring and glowed gently in the amber setting. Mercy had saved your love, the love that you would have let go, and still did let go at the end of it all.

"But my friend was dead. Was that not enough for you? My friend, the father whose fatherless son would grow up in ignorance of his true roots; whose dead father would never see the infant smile or the innocent tear. Tell me, was it not enough for you?"

One for you and one for me? Still not fair, is it? I wanted both of them, and to see you hate yourself for what you had done. The folly of your words with God, they saved your little one; the false promises and the glorious repentance, they eased my desire; the irony of your guilt, it was my tragic feed. 'I love her', you said, 'I did not mean it', you lied, 'I will look after her, please let her live, I am sorry, I am sorry', you prayed. And all the while your friend twitched, his feet dangling above your head while you sat clutching your love, your guilt, my tragedy.

"No more, muse, I must finish this chapter now, before you drive me mad again. I know your tricks. I know them. Go now, I shall not speak to you. I shall finish this incident now."

~

That term finished. People left, some stayed. Scarlet stayed, to continue another course; Jade moved on, to where I do not know. I returned home, back to the hidden and secret problems which I had discovered resided in our house, alongside us all. I spent many evenings at the cliffs and by the beach, and, of course, I don't even need to tell you now, those evenings when the moon was full and the sea was calm were my favourite. I would sit close to the water's edge, as far as I dared scramble down in the half-light. Ripples made by the wind, or perhaps by some hidden entity beneath the surface, sung to my imagination, and I would try to think of romantic verses full of beautiful mermaids; but always the lines ended in tragedy. The muse was gorging herself upon these couplets, at my sanity's expense. My reclusive nature was almost complete and once the initial shock of recent events was over, I would settle down to write the poems of pain which would feed the muse to the extent of its satisfaction.

But tragedy once more was about to unfold; it appeared that the muse was not quite ready for me. Perhaps, it thought, the gamble was fit for another stake before the cards were seen; a further round to push the poet to his limits, to test my madness and prime my verse. A gamble which worked in the muse's favour, since I retained my soul and was not yet pushed over the beyond by this next crisis; and the verses, the verses, it was *à la carte* for the sprightly muse.

One night, in my pain and anger, I stood above a roaring Thomspon's bay and threw the vial I had once found there back into the sea. This particular relic did not seem to sit comfortably with the others. My troubles had begun the year when I had found that cursed piece of glassware and so I cast it far back from where it had come. I aimed at the sea, at the shadows playing in the waves before they crashed onto the rocks. My hatred focused upon the images I imagined the dancing shadows to be, Autumn pain, Amber burden or deserting Erasmus. Yet as I threw the cursed vial so I cursed my father for his sins and betrayal. It was my hate and my passion that destroyed him, for the next day, as I have already written, he was found at the bottom of those cliffs, having failed to return from his walk. He had told me he would try that path one day, to exercise 'the old legs'. And his soul, well, you know the rest already. His soul resides with the mermaids now, in that glass vial, captured by the playful muse. But, one day, one day I shall free him again, and we shall seek each other's forgiveness, and on that day I will laugh out loud, and roar at the night sky and curse the muse since she still will lie trapped in her deep sea-cave.

"Amber, is that you?" The ring felt warm upon my finger. I had worn it since the day of her accident. "Is that you? I can see you." I turned, sweating in my bed. The dream was touched with reality.

"I'm here." It was a ghostly whisper, long and drawn, almost silent, but audible to my ears.

"How I've missed you. My father, you remember I told you, do you know what's happened, it's terrible..."

"Hush, little poet, I hear you, it's okay, it's going to be all right.

I'm right here with you, my dear."

My troubled eyes flicked open and shut, adjusting to the dawning light as it peered tentatively through coupled curtains. I awoke from my dream, as I would from such dreams for the coming months. Amber visited me regularly, small-talking in my sleep, trying to comfort my aching heart, trying to discover how Hate had dealt her such a savage blow. Slowly she would learn about the muse and its evil passage through my life. Within the confines of the magical ring I wore upon my finger, my little Amber would cogitate upon the existence of the strange and wonderful creatures of my life. Her mind would sit with me by the cliffs and cast stones at the teasing mermaid-shadows that broke the still of the sea; she would feel the passion in my heart as the muse bit me, she would witness the fickle reality of my soul and its quest for love and desire. What other person, except for perhaps the muse, could have known me better during those years? And at the end of each dream, she kissed me gently upon the head, as she had done that night I had broken her love.

"Muse, I am done now, the chapter is finished. Are you ready for the next?"

Your pain is my pain, remember that.

"Yet, I take no pleasure from my pain."

Do you really believe that, dear poet? I feel that perhaps I get the blame for more than I deserve. A father crippled and dumb because of your curse, an unrequited lover comatose because of your weaknesses. These are not my doing.

"I do not dwell in my own tragedy; no longer, dear muse. You and I, we are both to blame for the tragedies."

But we both know that you used to love and dwell in them. You used to wallow in the pain; it fed you as well as I, did it not?

"I thought I did, but now I prefer to blame it on you, and purify my soul before God judges me. I believe not that I once - what do you say? - 'wallowed', in these events."

...As Adam blamed Eve?

"But, I will be more convincing than Adam, for I truly believe it myself; and I shall be allowed to retain my paradise."

And I?

"Don't worry, I shall visit you, often. I have said it already. Now sleep; shall we sing?"

No, not tonight. I shall pleasure my mermaid friends with verses of old, for sometimes I am afraid that you will never release me from this deep sea-cave, and so my spirit will be entombed with these witches of the sea forever.

"You continue with your plans, dear muse, and tomorrow we shall carry on with the medicine, then you will sleep for a long, long time. Good night."

9

I discovered a fairy once, living at the bottom of my garden. I am afraid to tell you that I stamped on it, and killed it. I recall it very well indeed. It was sitting under a sprig of mint and pointing up at me and laughing as much as seemed possible for such a small creature. It annoyed me intensely and so I killed it. Perhaps you will forgive me for such an atrocity. Well, he was so young, you may say; he didn't realise what it was, you could consider; he was afraid, you would forgive. Well, I will tell you that I was afraid, but I knew what it was, very well I knew what it was. And as for the other excuse. Well, it happened only yesterday as I sat in the garden to write some notes for today's chapter.

So, I expect that you won't forgive me, which is fine for it is not your forgiveness that I seek, it is your attention, and no more than that.

My father lies in his bed in the hospital, because he is a liar. My precious Amber talks to me in my sleep from her sleep. I have two companions now who keep both of my shoulders warm, the muse upon one, my precious little one upon the other, though they are unable to see each other for my monstrosity of a head is in the way. I think that they sense another is there, for sometimes I can feel them trying to scurry round and take a peek, but they always seem to do it at the same time and so miss each other completely. How strange, don't you think? How odd that they should live so close yet never see each other?

Well, the muse has seen enough of my precious and that is fine, she need not be bothered by the muse's designs, not while she lies in the amber setting which I carry always upon my finger. But, O how

I think of beautiful Mercy when I wear that ring, what sweet catastrophe has fate laid upon her? Alone and parentless fate has now left her. Will all those around me suffer as she has and my other friends have? How delightful the conflict? Hmmm. I agree. It is not in the least enviable, despite what words Erasmus might have spun me. And now he is not even here to do that. Muse, how much do you require of me?

And so, in the muse's silence I shall continue this tale, from where I left off, so that you may know it all.

I spent the dying weeks of the summer mostly in my garden. It was sheltered from the wind, you understand, and I could sit and do nothing. For nothing was all I could do. And I was ashamed of it, or would be ashamed of it now. It was so uncreative, I realise, but very necessary at that particular time. For inside of me there was brewing, amidst all of the conflicts and the troubles, a set of poems, to 'enhance the hour and make light the burden.' Those were the words of encouragement that the muse would sometimes feed me, subconsciously when I felt the need to complain at the morbidity of my pen and verse as it lay on the pages and scrap pieces of paper, telling of my woes in a rhyming tongue. 'How does it work?' I would ask myself. 'Why am I doing this?' Sensible questions, of course. Midnight brandies often started me off doing my nothingness as I lay upon the floor of our lounge, scribbling, doodling, creating nothingness but for a few lines. But slowly these lines would come together and suddenly the nothingness would become somethingness. Perhaps not such a waste. But, yes they were. What waste were these songs for me and me alone to read, what price had I to pay to write a few verses with passion? 'To enhance the hour', of course. Oh no. No, no, no, no, no. The equation did not work, see: Pain + Sorrow = Tragedy – Sanity = Passion / Muse + Poet

= Sonnet Relief. The whole thing just did not add up. The quality of one hour was not worth a lifetime's suffering, unless it was for love of course, and if for love, then why not for hate? *Why not for hate?* No, I cannot make myself understand. Well, I could not, at the time. But I do now, since I am in full possession of the facts, and the muse. I am trying to make it easy for you, dear reader, to understand.

So write I did, I traded my sorrow for passion and my creativity for verses and soon I came to finish my little book of sonnets which I had started earlier. A slightly philosophical stance they had now acquired as well, perhaps reflecting the maturation of the muse, like a fine wine or possibly a festering illness. And soon, very soon, the summer came to an end. There was no improvement in my father's condition. 'Good', I feel bad now for saying it, but felt noble at the time. I made a courtesy visit to the bedside of my precious Amber's crumpled body, battered and twisted as it was. And I smiled as I saw her, because I knew that she lived with me, happily as could be. But, her parents were pleased to see me and to hear my story about the situation in person, boring though that version was compared to the elusive truth. I still needed to work hard to find the truth, oh yes.

And life presented itself to me. I took a job in the library, just working in the evenings, re-shelving the books at first, but this task would grow, and it was a task which I actually enjoyed. I started at around six in the evening and finished at ten, when the building was locked for the night. Part time work for a part time poet and a full time tragic hero. (By 'hero' I do not mean a man of great action, but rather a man against whom great actions happen.) After a little while I was trusted enough at work to lock the doors myself, they knew me there anyway, and it was just a small local library. I was a suitable part time caretaker. How I loved it. It was part of my medicine, the muse's tonic to be precise. But bitter was the lemon and the gin was poison. Alone at night-time: just me, the books, the muse, and Amber.

~

I have danced with the devil in the light of the moon when it shines full upon the sea, through a thin curtain of ghostly cloud. I have waltzed hand in hand with the beast upon the precipice of a rocky pediment… and I did not cast him into the sea, lest his strength was greater than mine and I should be the tumbling one. Perhaps I should have been more courageous and fought the creature, though I doubt I would have won, for courage is an unreliable soul. And how I would hate to tumble down those sharp and punishing crags to my death, to be torn apart by their anger and sent to a watery grave with the mermaids in the sea below. What a hateful death is that to me, who has now so much happiness beside him. But as happiness rests in her bed, I must continue the tale.

At first I thought it not possible to kill a ghost, but it can be done. There are special ways and means to kill the dead. This was part of the inspiration which ignited this tale; 'to kill a muse', I should have named it. Have you guessed that yet? Yes, one must punish the soul of the departed until it mourns so deeply for what it can no longer have that it fades away and expires, until the spirit is no more. Then I do not know what happens to it, all I know is that it is gone and shall trouble you no more. "Is that not so, muse?" *That it is, that it is*. And, should we then attempt to kill the greatest ghost of all – our Dear Lord? Of course we shouldn't, but we should ask Him to justify His little world a little more before He expects us all to behave rationally. I will not try to kill any ghosts other than the muse, but I will tell a story to question the Lord as I question the muse… I am afraid that this deep and ill-founded thinking was the product of too much enclosure by books, the living thoughts of authors dead and alive pervaded my sanity.

There was once a man. I think that you have probably heard of him. His name was Jesus. He had other names, you know of whom I am talking. Now, this man whom many millions now follow made me think, too much. And that was my undoing. As my life matured into chaos I looked for an answer. Of course, I have learnt now that one should first seek the question.

Religion was flawed, far too flawed to comfort my situation and so still the tragic verse flowed, provoked by my listening friend. And these were the tales, the songs, of this moment.

Time for a song now?

"Not just yet, it's coming."

The tale of the woman who had sinned, an affair was it that she had? The story from the Bible, I hope you know the one I mean. 'Let he who has never sinned, let he be the one to cast the first stone.' Were those the words? Should it not have been 'Let He who has never sinned, let He be the One to cast the first stone.' Dear reader, do you, like the muse and I, now see the difference?

Tell them; shall I do it for you?

Was Jesus at that time not guilty of a great sin? What good is a lawmaker who does not pursue His Own aims? What good is justice with no Judge to implement it? What is a hypocrite? O Lord, were You not there, at that place, watching and preaching to those men with stones ready in their hands? Were You not there as they faltered at Your words and let the sinner live? Were You not free of sin dear Lord? Why did You not cast that first stone?

Don't answer me now, please don't answer me now. This is a message for my readers.

You see, the world is more than simply the poet and I. It is greater than just the muse and his poor friend. There are also decisions and poems for you to make and write. Do not be fools and forget the importance of sin. I am sin. I have made you think. I have answered your questions before, even, you have asked them of me.

"Enough, muse. The readers are mine, you shall not speak to them."

O but the last words shall be mine, to them; you shall see, they shall see. Don't forget now, don't forget.

"Now I shall put a sonnet to shut you up."

And what shall it be?

"I must continue the story, but first some words of thought for you."

You call upon the pure to be the first
To be the marksmen for the sentence due,
Command the mob – restrain their bloody thirst,
Until some taintless soul so heads their cue.
"Let he who's free from sin be first to cast".
Your clever words push conscience on the crowd,
And make their stone-filled hearts reflect their pasts,
Of which I see, not one of them is proud.
Yet One I know Who should not now depart,
Who should not drop His stone unto the ground,
Should be the One to cue the stoning start,
Who by His words is now to justice bound…
Since You my Lord are surely free from sin,
And so should You this punishment begin.

And there I continued, my little life fated to spend the next year being cursed by thoughts so foolish and perverted, so unusual, so not normal. Why could I not just have led a normal and muse free existence? I do not have this answer. It was not until I met my wife that I thought I had finally shaken the muse and put an end to her curse. But now I am almost caught up with my current life. I have yet to tell of my saviour who became my wife, and I am required to instruct you as to how to discover the muse, in case you should fall ill to the same fate as me. And I have finally to tell you how I fought and trapped the little sprite in her deep sea-cave.

There would be a fight. There would be an awful fight, and it would happen so very soon. It still panics me to think of the ferocity with which the muse fought me that night. But it panics me even more to think of the hate and the aggression which spilled forth from me as we grappled and struck at each other in those freezing and stormy waters.

But before this would happen I had to realise the true nature of the muse, that it was even there at all. And this would occur one night on my journey home from work.

I had locked up at the library as usual and was walking back through town when an elderly gypsy lady, whom I had never in fact seen round these streets before, came up to me and asked, "your future for a cup of tea, little one?"

"No thanks," I replied, though I was happy to pay the price for a cup of tea on this cold night, so I did stop and reach into my pocket for change.

"Triumphant you will be, though struggle you must my precious spirit."

"Sorry?" I looked strangely at the old woman as I pulled a few coins from my pocket. My breath turned to fog and blew across the old woman's eyes as she stared at my shoulder and continued her speech.

She laughed and smiled, as though listening to a joke, and continued "very well, my child, feed well and be happy."

I tried to attract the attention of this mad woman who was entirely oblivious to my every action. Just as I was about to turn away she reached out and clutched my hand before I could pull it back. She stared at me, right through my eyes, her gaze cold and petrifying. She placed her other hand underneath the hand of mine she had grasped, which she turned so that the change fell into her clutches. After looking down and counting it silently, she looked again at me, knowingly and mercifully.

"Beware the pain you carry my son, beware the cradle you have made for that devil child. Beware the future, my boy. Get rid of that thing you hold upon your shoulder, that beast which haunts you and will haunt you forever lest you give up your tragic lust."

And then she let go and left, walking along the street into the night. I watched her go until she turned the corner and I could no longer see her. I stood frozen, still watching, my mouth hanging in unreason.

And then something else very peculiar happened. I got run over by a young woman riding her bike along the pavement.

We awoke a few hours later that evening, both of us in the hospital. I had fallen and bumped my head against a lamp post while she had injured herself likewise on the concrete paving slabs below us. But when we woke, we had known each other a lifetime, for we had sat in the ambulance together and talked and talked and talked while we both stared at our amusingly dumb and slightly bloodied bodies. I had first seen our bodies lying there when the accident first occurred, in fact the more I think about it the more I think that I actually saw my body standing there cold and lonely before she even ran into me. It was 'of course' entirely her fault, as she fought between stopping at the fast food restaurant she had just passed or continuing on her way. With her head turned to catch the special of the day plastered in the window she was helpless to see me, and I her, as I stared the other way after my mysterious bringer of tidings, the gypsy lady.

After the collision I crouched down to try to tend to my fallen body, when I heard a voice from behind me. "I'm really sorry about that." It was weak and hesitant and so polite. It was beautiful. When I first heard her speak I knew that I would ask this woman to be my wife. I turned to see her and she stood there, her spirit fading in and out of time as I suppose my own was doing. Our bodies fought to retain their spirits, surprised at being sent unconscious by such a feeble knock. We introduced ourselves, showing the utmost courtesy for each other. I felt truly a real gentleman and was pleased that at this moment in my life I had tried to behave as one, for here, before me, was suddenly a beauty, a lady, who should not be tainted or ill-treated.

It was not long before an ambulance arrived and carried away our bodies. The ambulance crew seemed unduly worried that such slight external injuries had resulted in two rather deep concussions. They tried to revive us at first, but soon gave up and took us in to the hospital. Her name was Ariadne, but I would call her Ariane.

I helped Ariane into the back of the already moving ambulance, our spirits gliding along with our thoughts as we wished ourselves where we wanted to be.

I shall not bore you with the details of the conversations we had that evening, an evening which really did seem as though it lasted a lifetime. We cemented some very important foundations. I suppose that the most important discovery I made next to this new love was as I returned to my body. I had sat and watched it for a long time now but had not noticed until I stood and walked closer to it, as Ariane did so with hers, that something was slumbering and stirring by my head. I looked more closely as I moved in. This object did not appear in the same hazy light as did the other souls and structures around me. This thing was sharp and concise, as though it belonged in this world, the ghostly and foggy spirit world. Whilst my own self drifted from light to dark and from form to form, this thing was almost real, in a world which was not real. I got closer and saw what had attached itself to my shoulder. Terrified I was to return to my own body after I saw it, but unable to stop the pull of it. I was sucked back in, like vapour being inhaled. The last vision I recall was the slumbering beast, claws sunk into my shoulder and extending deep inside my flesh, rooted towards my heart. An evil, yet seductive, face carried the beast off as something more than evil, giving it character and beauty. Panic set itself within me and, as my eyes flicked open and I regained consciousness, I struck at my shoulder with my fist, only to dent the soft pillow upon which my sore head lay.

Mystified and scared I stared up at the ceiling.

"So you're awake then. At long last."

"How are you finding the story, dear muse?"

We are now very nearly there, I see.

"Yes. The game is almost done."

Have you ever wondered why people can be so evil sometimes? How they can suck, like parasites, upon the spirit of life itself, do you ever wonder?

"I have thought of some people as, not evil, but not good people. I do not consider that evil is the absence of good. Where is your questioning taking me anyway?

I wonder how you can lock me up in this deep sea-cave for all of eternity.

"It is where you belong."

Only in your world; in some worlds people thrive on me, they love me, they love the pain I bring and the games I play. Don't you ever love me? No, of course not, not now that you have your wife. Do not bore the readers, dear poet, with the rest of the story, that is not what you are here to teach them.

"But perhaps the most important lesson is just that: how to fall in love, I mean really fall in love. Though I don't believe that one can work that out; you need the right match in the first place."

Whatever you say, poet. You are the boss. You are the one who no longer needs me now, who is in love. You have forsaken your Autumn lost and your Amber dear. You no longer wish that the lovely Mercy was your Autumn fresh... perhaps that would have been a good match for you after all...

"I no longer needed you, you are right. We were married quickly, we both knew that it was the right thing to do, there was no reason not to. But then, that is the time I began to fear you. I had seen your form, crawling all over me like the lecherous parasite you speak of, sucking away my life."

I only wanted to sing a song with you, a song of sadness.

"I was right to do what I did, to expose your form and drown you beneath the depths."

As you keep saying... so you keep justifying yourself. But I am still confident.

"And I still fear you, while I hear you in my head. That is why I must finish this work, and kill your spirit in that deep sea-cave. Your spirit is what I fear the most in life. But, this story will be the end of you. I will torture you with the stories of our tales, and as you realise your fate, as you see that you can play no more, you will dwindle and disappear for ever."

You had better hope so dear poet, for if I ever escape from here I shall come for you, and we shall make tragedy one more time. Enough now of our bickering. Continue the story. You are married, yes? I think that is the point at which you intend to re-join the tale, no?

"If you wish. It is as good as anywhere. We are married and in love, and happy. The tragedy has gone from my life, but the fear has not. I have seen you now and realised that it is you who brings the sadness into my life, so that you can write with me these awful sonnets. I recognise your thirst and I fear that you have set me up for the ultimate loss, the loss of true love. So my story is now at a place where I must plan your demise. And pay attention especially now, dear reader, so that should the muse ever favour you, then you will know the course that you should take."

It happened in a dream one night, as I lay next to Ariane. The night air crept freshly through the window, caressing the curtains as it entered. I slept deeply, dreaming, a special dream. I dreamt that I was walking through a terrible corridor of twisted branches and entwined creepers. It was a monstrosity of nature, a gateway to hell which lay in some far off forest of my mind. I was searching painfully for a way out of this labyrinth, more and more eager to escape as I heard the noises and haunting sounds that I could ascribe to no particular source. Fear began to mount up within me, but then I found a small shred of hope in the darkness. I saw ahead of me a silvery, shining cord, floating in the air and leading a way through the passages. I followed this ghostly cord, which wrapped its swirling mistiness around me as I raced through it, following its every twist and turn. It comforted my heart and I saw light ahead. It was the end of the passage. And there was my lovely Ariane. But as I reached her open arms and my heart filled with love, love and joy, I turned my head and looked with a tear in my eye at the closing darkness that had been my haunt. No longer would I yearn for escape from those dank passages, no more would my pulse race as I fought the evil that lay within the dark woods. No more would I feel the sadness which troubled me so. But, also, no more would I pass through my busy mind the lines and verses of sonnet tragedy. No more would those soft and beautiful lines ease a troubled hour. No more would the gentle rhyme caress my sore body. No more would the flowing easiness of complex feelings be admired. My Ariane had led me to safety, and to freedom from the haunting muse. I would miss her. I felt my shoulder in the dream, and it was free from the monster that I had witnessed during my unconsciousness in the hospital.

I awoke from the dream. I looked over to the clock which glowed an early hour to me. Darkness and stillness occupied the present. I carefully and slowly lifted myself from my bed, unusually full of energy from my dream.

I crept out of the room and let my eyes drift over my sleeping wife, content that she, at least, was sleeping soundly and peacefully.

I went down the stairs of our house and out into the garden. We had bought the house soon after we were married. It was quiet and away from the business of the town. Outside the clouds were lit by the full moon in their race to who knows where. Consistently and speedily they drifted along in the fresh night breeze. I breathed in the beauty of the cold night air. I filled my lungs with the stillness of what would soon be disturbed by the waking of others and the beginning of that day's tasks.

I sat down on a dew-covered bench outside, first placing a kitchen towel to protect me from the dampness. I shut my eyes and continued breathing slowly and steadily, trying to fall into some form of meditation.

It was then that they came. First I noticed the glow of dancing flames beckoning my eyelids to open, which they did to satisfy curiosity. And, indeed, there was a small fire lit in the middle of our garden. But, that was not the first thing which I saw. The first thing I saw was my two old friends sitting beside this fire. Amber and Erasmus Wallace sat on the grass beside the fire, looking at me, clearly waiting for me to approach them. In disbelief I got up and went over to them.

As I stood over them, about to say something, Amber turned her smile away from me and looked at Erasmus. Erasmus returned her knowing look and silently stood and took hold of my hand. The second he did so we rose up into the air and took to the still night like spirits. The most fantastic experience of my life followed as we flew through the curtain of night, allowing its smooth silkiness to caress our forms, his ghostly and mine corporeal. Even Erasmus, dead as I knew he was, smiled across his face a thrill inexplicable except to those who have experienced something similar.

Across the countryside and the town we flew, the twinkling lights below seemingly flashing their admiration at our joy. And then down we came to the beach, to Thompson's Bay. Erasmus placed me down on the rocks underneath the cliffs to the side of the beach. He looked at me, no longer smiling, but now more purposefully. I looked back at him, into the eyes of my dear lost friend.

His eyes turned and stared straight ahead as he raised an arm and extended a finger. I followed the line of his gaze into the cave ahead of us. I knew that he wanted me to enter. Holding my fear easily because of the wonderment of the situation, I walked boldly into the sea-cave. A glow filled the sea-cave so that I could see what I needed to find. A short way in there was a rock projected from the floor and upon it sat a small glass vial. *I recognise you,* I thought to myself. I looked at the glass vial and walked out of the cave, knowing that on this occasion I was to venture no further into the jealous realms of the mermaids, nor was I to take any further action. I exited the sea-cave and without a word Erasmus lifted me high into the air. As we returned I knew that the spirit of my father now lay in that glass vial and that the cursed muse had caused him to be there. Seeing the scene in the sea-cave gave me two things. It gave me realisation and it gave me forgiveness. I forgave my father immediately for all the hurt and pain that had been caused, and I hoped that he could forgive me for all of the hate that I had cast against him. Together I felt that we now stood, he and I against the passionate squeeze of the cursed muse.

I knew that one day he would rise from the dumb chair in which he now sat and he would look me in the eye, and one more time we would sit and talk about unimportant things. My heart was filled with joy. And my heart was filled with realisation. I must release my precious Amber. I no longer needed this friend upon my shoulder, her heart beating warm within the ring which now had been placed in a closed and locked drawer in my house. I should now release her from the sadness of my life to which I had tied her; I could live now without her support. Suddenly I knew what I had to do.

Erasmus brought us home safely. The fire was burning low and Amber lay cuddled up as close to it as she could, her eyes in a half sleep from which she awoke swiftly on seeing us home. She looked first at me, then at Erasmus, then back at me. I approached her and knelt facing her. I took her ghostly hand and raised it to my lips, kissing it gently.

"Thank you" I whispered, "but the fight is now mine and you should look to yourself, my dear love."

I kissed her hand once more and she disappeared, fading slowly into the growing dawn. When she had completely vanished I stood and I knew that my friend Erasmus would be gone too. Once again I had not said goodbye to him. I turned to confirm my thought.

"Good luck, my old friend. Thank you for showing me forgiveness. I'm sorry that I shan't see you again." I spoke into the dawn air and vapour from my mouth danced and twisted in front of me. Then I awoke, back in my bed, next to my wife, as though nothing had happened.

But it had happened. The next morning I called Amber's parents and was not surprised to hear their ecstatic voices as they told me that she had woken from her coma. I look forward to the time when I shall next see my old friend and we shall share stories of our adventures.

I knew also of the vial, hidden away in the sea-cave. I knew that one day I would have to smash that vase and release the spirit of my father. But most importantly I had realised that to do this I must destroy the foul spirit that had written this tragedy. I must close the tangled forest of its dark and tragic existence for good. I must not allow myself to be the source of its food any longer. I must turn the tables and destroy this spirit. I would over-feed the muse. I would choke her fragile throat upon the cursed verse which she so loved. I would watch her struggles as she tried to catch her breath in the icy, chilled waters of tragic poetry. And when I was sure that her spirit was finished, I would release my life from the turmoil of her poetry.

And I would do this soon, before she could do more harm to me or my family.

"Muse. Do you think that it is dangerous to love something too much?"

Yes, of course, for you especially, my precious. And look where it has got me. My love for tragedy. No. My fate *for tragedy has left me isolated and at destruction's door amidst the hollows of this cave. But you speak of your lovely wife, do you not?*

"I do. I speak of her and still I worry that one day you may rise yet from your cave and seek us out."

You are not so sure of your final verse then, dear poet. You are not sure that you could kill my spirit, is that what you are saying?

"I am saying that I am tired, dear muse. I am tired of fighting you, and if I fail or stop now I want to know if you would come after me and try to take the life of my beloved. Would you try to make me write another tragic verse, one so beautiful that it far surpassed anything you had ever heard before? Would you do that, muse? Would you come after me?"

Yes, dear poet. Yes I would.

"That is what I feared. Good night muse."

Good night poet.

10

Take the notes and memories of your past and bury them beneath the waterline on the lowest ebb of the month, when the wind is bitter and the elements are alive. Take the feathers of the winged beasts and the diamond tears that fell from my sad eyes. Take the amber ring, which once held she who was dear to you but who now walks again. Take the hate which you have now put aside for forgiveness, take the longing of first and lost loves and all of the bitterness which slid down your cheeks. Take all of these things and bury them true and well, and let none see you as you do this or they too will be cursed, as curse you will the muse. But, above all, take those wretched lines that you have written upon those pages black. Take your books of sonnets tragic and put them at the bottom of the hole which you will make in the sand beneath the waterline.

When you are done, stand fast and think of nothing. Then you will have won the battle, my dear brother, my brother dear, then you will have won the battle, for I will come down and stand by your side one last time. I will look to make sure that you have buried the tools of the muse and I shall command that she appears. She will not refuse me, my brother. She will come and then you shall have your battle, and you will win.

There is no other way, my brother dear, trust me. Take hold of her when she appears and put her head beneath the rising tide. Hold her down and think not that she is lovely or that she is beautiful. Do not relinquish your grip as the surf crashes around your cold feet. Hold her whilst she struggles and chants at you. Feed her with the tragic verse with which she has cursed your life and gorged herself. Feed her well and true, my brother. Feed her until those eyes stop touching your heart, pleading for pity. Drown her until there is no more life in that body. And when you are done I shall carry her unto the deep sea-cave and I shall leave her there. And you, my brother dear, I shall leave you too, forever this time. I shall miss you.

"Wake up."

"What?"

"You were talking in your sleep. Are you okay? It's time for work, you'll be late."

"Okay. I know. I know. I know what I have to do. You go back to sleep, sweetness."

~

Black was the night that I gathered up the remnants of memories to be forgotten, as my not-brother had instructed me. I was sad that this night would mean I would never see him again, even though I thought he had been lost long since. Now I knew that he would be lost. But as for being sad about destroying the muse… I was not sad. I wanted peace now. Perhaps in the future I would miss the tragedy which I was about to bury. But, those thoughts are for another time and for another story. I shall not dwell here on the ethics of loss and the sympathy of happiness and tragedy, and whether or not they are one and the same thing. No, the story is now at an end and I shall return you to that fateful evening where we began. Remember the first lesson I taught you dear reader: … take heed, when you stand alone upon an empty cliff, above a roaring sea, with the moon casting a beckoning path of light towards the open ocean. Beware of those distant stars that carry strange demons within their light. Shun the midnight breeze as it dances and sings around your body. And, if you should look upon the deep blue, where the whiteness lashes the rocks, and see there figures diving and leaping, then know that danger is upon you.

I took myself and my collection of items including, most importantly the books which I had treasured, those little books of sonnets. I went forth into the blackness of the night, into the wind and the rain and I climbed down the cliffs to Thompson's Bay. I struggled and clambered over the rocks onto the sand of the beach, my eyes squinting against the wind-driven rain and the surf that lashed its sting across my naked face.

I walked down to the water's edge where the wind howled over the crashing waves that soaked my legs. Down I sank and pulled away chunks of sand with my hands. The water rolled back over where I had dug and filled in the hole that I would never be able to dig properly. But I persevered and, as the waves subsided for a rest between sets, I pulled from my pockets the items I needed to bury and stuffed them into the sand, pushing them as deep as I could into the wetness so that they were covered. This would do, and I pulled my sinking feet out of the water's edge and stood back, clearing my mind.

I watched the sea in front of me, its dark expanse beckoning and threatening at the same time. I watched hard to see what I could in the darkness. There was nothing, but I knew that she would come, as I stared and thought about this nothingness.

And then I felt a hand rest upon my shoulder and I heard the sweetest and softest of voices in my ear.

"What are you doing?"

It was my wife. She had followed the emptiness of her bed to the place where she knew she would find me. She had clambered down the same cliffs, seeing me a short way in front of her as she reached the sand. She had watched as I fought to dig in the sand. She had come with comfort and love in her heart, but O how I trembled at the thought of what she now might find.

"Nothing, my precious." I looked with sadness and pity in my eyes.

As I reached out my hands to hold her waist I fell backwards into the sea, whilst she was knocked back towards the beach. An exceptionally large wave had rolled its way towards us, hidden by the noise of the wind. Whilst Ariane was knocked to the sand on the beach, I was taken down and under the waves, pulled by clutching claws at my heels, claws which showed an evil pair of glowing eyes behind them.

And there I was... my sweetness.

"And there you were, dear muse."

How beautifully you have told the tale. So well, I have thought to myself.

"I have not quite finished."

O I think that will do. We fought and we cursed and we struggled and we did all that; nothing really.

"Perhaps not for you, but for me it was an evening I shall never forget, especially while your voice still haunts me from that deep sea-cave. I cursed you, my muse. I gripped your hands tight as you tried to drag me deeper and deeper into the water. I reached for the surface, for the lash of wind upon my face and the freshness of air into my lungs. Like you I took a deep breath, and then plunged into the stormy waters. But, I suppose that you are not used to the corporeal form you had taken are you, muse dear? Now you know how it feels."

It was not unpleasant. Your eyes and your heart have not changed since you held my body. We could not see each other in the dark, but you felt me go limp and the struggling ceased. I remember the verses that went through your mind as you chanted and wished me to die.

"You died almost too easily that night, little muse. I did feel for you as I felt your body float away into the waters. I felt your hands leave mine as my wife pulled me from the ever deepening waters. Our fingertips were the last to part. And then you were gone. Taken to the depths."

Shall we chant the lines again?

"Yes we will, and then you shall be gone forever. I shall rest once more before I finish this story and I shall enjoy the day tomorrow before we talk for the final time. We shall write the lines one last time for the readers, the verses which we sang to each other under those dark rolling waves. And I pray that those last precious verses, when you hear them once again, will kill your spirit as they drowned your body. I pray that the mermaids will seal the embers of your soul inside that deep sea-cave so that never more may man be touched by your tragic heart. And most of all, I thank God that He has now made things right between you and me, dear muse, that now I can once again live a normal and peaceful life. It is good to fear God, my muse. I wish that you had learnt this. But, how my life has tricked Him, with Himself on the one hand and you on the other. How can this be? Come now, it is time to sleep."

Then sleep well, my poet dear, and enjoy your day. I love you. I have always loved you, my dear poet since the dawn of all creation. You were the best of them, you truly were, and I shall sing the verses tomorrow alongside you, once more for old time's sake. Just you and I, dear poet. Then you may rest. Then you may put down your pen and leave your little office, go and sit with your wife and perhaps read a book. All I ask is that once in while on a smooth, still night when the moon is full and the fishes are leaping from the water as the mermaids chase them; all I ask is that you go down to the place above where we fought and that you say a prayer for me. I hope that God will not be too angry with me. Will you do that for me, dear poet? Will you? Will you end it there as well, my poet? Will you bring your verses and sing them to me one last time at that place above the cliffs? Will you sit in the light of the setting sun and repeat them over and over to me softly and softly until you can feel me no more, until the light is out and the spirit has stopped burning. O to watch a thing die is such a privilege, O so beautiful can death be. Please come, dear poet, and sit upon the cliffs. Come down and be happy that tomorrow I shall find my rest. I think that you have been right all this time. Tomorrow I shall rest, and you shall sing me to sleep. And when it is done you shall take the warm hand of your wife and walk happily home.

"I will. Now sleep, dear muse, and dream."

Good night dear poet, don't forget to pray for me after it is done.

"I will not, my dear muse. I will not forget." Good night my dear muse. I shall miss you.

Epilogue

"It is left to me, the cursed muse, the tale's villain, to tell of the end. I suppose that surprises you, doesn't it? It is a good ending. He came down to send me to sleep forever. He came down to finish me, to finish me gently but to finish me for good. He looked forward to those nights when he could look down into the waters and say a prayer for me. That was not how it was meant to be, he being allowed to remember our happy times in prayer and recollection whilst I felt nothing but emptiness in non-existence.

He came armed with happiness and he came full of life. Murder was not the least in his mind, not until the seconds before he died.

"But it was quick, mind you. Do not be sad or fretful, it was humane. I did not hold him in the icy water as he held me. I did not store him in any deep sea-cave of mine. But down he came, alone he was not. Happiness was with him, she walked beside him. That wife of his, so beautiful you know, so pretty. What a tragic waste that I could never rest my hands on her. We cannot touch those already cursed, you know. Yes, down he came. Armed with happiness, to kill me, you realise, to destroy me. Happiness would have destroyed me, to see them sitting there on our rocks, on our disfigured plain where once we had written such tragic verse it delights my heart beyond meaning to recall the very language of the thing.

"O pity me not, I do not expect it of you, he has told you all from his view, not what it feels like to be a spirit like myself. But he will understand now, now that he is no more. And yes, also, one day, one day you will understand.

"Down he came. I had escaped from my deep sea-cave. It is a little known fact that once a year the mermaids gather at a certain place, near India so they say, in the Indian Ocean, and there

they watch the breaking of one new dawn a year. Every year. Well, now you know, I trust you will not make the same mistake. "Lock the doors, they forgot... Haaaaaa... Lock the chains, they forgot... Hmmmmm. Yes. Wondrous day of new light, what tragedy you have brought upon my poet dear, upon my poet dead. A display of light so fantastic. Thank you dawn.

"Running he came down, ahead of happiness, so full of life, so bright, having nearly finished his tale; the last chapter ready to be written at the end of that day; ready to tell of my final demise. We had only our little verses of happiness to go, so he came to send me to sleep, to sing me to sleep forever, and then to close the book of poetry. So gently he had planned it all... I had planned it all.

Running, jumping, leaping steps on the steep downward passage to the beach. Why not? So many times he had carried heavy burdens upon his shoulders to this place, he knew every rock, every step, every trip. But he did not know that I awaited him at the bottom. Ahead of happiness he ran, so very quickly, he ran. He turned for the final corner, and the final steps, looking to the beach and the rocks below, looking to the lovely spring day around him, so very few steps left before the sand, but enough... a drop is a drop, and there I was.

"He came running down to the beach armed with happiness and full of life. He turned and saw me sitting at the final corner, armed with terrible love. Up and fast I flew, screeching my tune to the king of the mermaids, 'I love him, I love him'... but there is no poet merman left for me.

"And do you know what she saw? All she saw was a rising gull, flapping its terrified wings, startled at the running poet. Arms flailing, gripping breaking bushes, tearing themselves on thorns, bashing themselves on rocks and... a short drop. That she did not see. Ooohh scream she did indeed. Run she did also, down to the scene of my crime, his crime. And there he lay, not on the

path but on the rocks below at the foot of the beach. A little fall but enough, armed with happiness he was! Well, it didn't do him much good, did it?

"Blood gently played down her cursed, cradling arms as she rocked his broken head back and forth against her chest, her lovely tear-stained chest. Her lovely hair knotted now with drying blood. That lovely soul who had seen what she should not see.

"But I too spared a tear for my lovely poet. I shall go and visit him soon, when he has checked in. And you, my friend. I feel like I've known you for years. You and I, we go back a long way you know, all the way to the beginning of the story. Well, you know everything about me, and now, once you have finished the last chapter for our dear departed poet, you must sit and tell me a story, a song for me, to feed me just a little. Will you do that, just for me? Will you, dear reader... reader dear?"

Come, come let us begin...

II

Love Sonnets

1

About thee girl do I see little Love,
You do not seek the passion of the gods,
But squirm and writhe in playful fits of lust,
Your lovers' hands upon your flesh gain nods
Of joy which answer every snaring quirk.
Your shape that shows those sinful curves malign,
Would they were spirits, O' in hell they'd lurk,
And rot to shameful dust when 'tis your time.
In you I see the girl I once did love,
The same whose care held dear; but yours does not.
I'll seek my truth by sea and rise above,
The passing of the waves will cleanse the spot,
And I, my dearest, I will now forget,
And cast once more my loving lovers' net.

2

Sun shine on me, for pale is my soul,
And darkness claims my every waking hour.
This place where meets the sea will make me whole,
And scenes of breathless grace will give me power.
Bright pearls upon the crested deep do flash,
Blue skies are paintings touched by hands divine,
The waves upon disfigured rocks do crash
Their timeless melody of notes so fine.
I feed upon the weightless thoughts of birds,
But always passion's curse doth feed my mind,
And mercilessly turns my thoughts towards
That sin of lust, where I will evil find.
Speak not, my muse, for now my soul's at war,
Your pleasant lines my feelings would abhor.

3

She holds my heart with teasing looks of love,
And steals away my soul without my leave;
The brightness of the skies and stars above
Is hers to grant to whom she'd choose to please.
O' muse upon my shoulder hear my plea:
This beauty holds my life within her price.
Be that the cost to love, I'd pay the fee,
Aboard my soul for trial I'd take this vice.
When love is born it wanes not like the moon,
Or shines anew with every tide of life;
To hell I'd never sink. To hear her tune
I'd stay upon the earth, make her my wife.
There'll grow a tree above our lover's grave,
Each other's soul our mortal love would save.

4

Unhappy sadness drops with every tear
From red-stained eyes that burn in sanguine hue,
The mirror shows that face I've grown to fear,
And now I've lost all chance of loving you.
Make me an offer of thy warmth, and touch
My heart with healing hands and looks so sweet
That I may feel the life I love so much
Once more before the next I leave to meet.
Dare you but kiss so soiled a flesh as mine
Or show your sex no bounds to beastliness?
My dream was once to make my looks divine,
But with each flaw my care grows less and less.
Now understand the life I've never led,
Mourn not for me, for I was always dead.

5

The saving of your soul would be my task,
A task to which I'd dedicate my life.
Your foes with sword I'd cut and slash with knife,
But know me not, for I should wear a mask,
My name I'll keep, so do not think to ask,
For when I've faced the trouble and the strife,
I'll not call you to be my mortal wife;
All thoughts of having you away I'd cast,
For beauty such as yours would ne'er be mine,
Your gentle hands would never touch my skin;
So do not waste your time and love on me -
If not I'd fought, my court you would decline.
Thus in the end 'tis you who really win,
For I'm too coy and lost to charge my fee.

6

I hunt amid the running pack of hounds,
The scent we trace boils blood thoughout our veins,
And those we chase, we'll laugh amid their pains;
And all this time I've known no other bounds
Save chasing tongues and captured sighing sounds.
I'd never thought to tear free from my reins,
Or live my life down less immoral lanes,
'Til you I caught one day on hunting grounds.
And now I'll turn my darkness into light,
Dispatch the hounds of hunting lust I will,
I'll clad in steel and take my holy knife,
Lift high my sword and ready for the fight;
And evil fiends for you I'll ever kill,
For you my princess are my only life.

7

Harsh sounding voices ring through midnight clear,
Consuming flames raise day into the night,
A gunshot soars and laces men with fear,
And rushing past are people lost in flight.
I look upon this land that I hold dear,
The fields I played in when I was a child,
The green-leafed trees that keep my memories near,
And deep blue seas that stir with waters mild.
But now the fields are bare and barren land,
The trees have fallen naked to the earth,
And bloody waves do break upon the sand,
For war has come to deal its bloody death.
So look you now, yes, you who caused this sin:
You've conquered nought but Satan's pleasing grin.

8

For you I'd die and cast my soul to hell,
I'd curse the face of every demon there,
I'd stride with ease the darkest ever fall,
And walk the blackest cave without a care,
For you I love, o tender of my heart;
I shed my tears each time I hear your name,
And brave myself to know again that hurt,
Our love was such to know eternal pain.
I'd sing to you the songs within my soul,
But laugh and joke, as though they were not true,
And you, my dear, you'd play a sim'lar role,
Play light your love and never follow through.
And now we sit, a thousand worlds apart,
So touching not, except within our hearts.

9

I met my princess once upon a time:
Her blue eyes flashed with midnight's moonlit charm,
Her voice with harps divine did make to rhyme,
And softness stirred about her gentle calm.
But she a princess walks upon this earth,
And I a hero, little more than that;
And so a prince she surely doth deserve;
Therefore my love I must not burden put.
I pray to God that there's a wife for me,
That one day I'll love more than I love thee,
Or else in life I'll never be set free,
For in my dreams I'll always picture thee.
And now my sweet, in every moonlight sky,
I'll speak your name 'til love unsung doth cry.

10

Distraught in temper's fiery glow I lay,
A troubled spirit breaks and rocks my mind,
This turbulence of thought will stay 'til day,
Unless in sweet converse I solace find.
And in the darkness slumber took its hold,
But be not sad that sleep my spirit took,
For darling dreams did in their arms me fold,
That with tired eyes I would not 'morrow look.
I dreamt I heard you call my name that night,
Your frightened voice from storms did shelter seek,
And with my strife I came and calmed your fright,
Healed you, my heart, when I did hear you speak,
And as I left I dreamt that I did spy,
A kiss from you, blown from your window high.

11

'Tis passion's burning heart that slows these lines,
And disallows my mind to work its course;
But now my love is eased towards that source,
So sharp I'll tease my soul with stirring rhymes.
O girl I pay for thee a grave-deep toll
That bleeds my lingering heart with jaws that gnaw;
Break the fast that hinders so your love or
Fast break my heart which searches for your soul.
And there I kill my passion's warm embrace,
Just like the times before which made me cold;
'Tis only when I'm cold that I am bold,
And in this mode, alone, my life I face.
But 'tis not courage makes the lovers' part,
'Tis more the fear of breaking their love's heart.

12

When soft you laid your head upon my chest,
Or when your greens did match my loving glaze,
And when your stay did hint of coupling ways,
These visions told my heart that I was blessed.
But in the space it took to fall for you,
So told was I that never could it be,
I'm just the shade and not the sheltering tree,
And wrong, I'm told, to harvest love so true.
But, oh, this messenger of words irate
Against her jealous heart did wish us well,
Unselfish thoughts to both her friends did tell;
Yet all along she knew the cupid's fate.
So, nought did come of all this love un-told,
And now my wondering heart must cease its hold.

13

If dreamers love do in their deep sleep find,
And lovers dream of loving when they wake,
Then let me sleep within my heart and mind
With dreams so real that dreaming lovers make.
For dreams of love do stir my daily thought,
And, living thus, I longing lovers seek,
But searching so brings not the love I sought,
To wake and find these loves I am too meek.
Smarten fast I must my troubled tale,
Else never will this aching leave my head,
Eternal loneliness would be to fail,
And none but dreams would share my empty bed.
While loving not I'll seek out passion's lot,
And pray I'll find and tie my lover's knot.

14

When kissing thee 'tis always in a dream,
Where shadows meet but bodies never lie.
Pronounced to thee my love has never been,
My lips so dry will stay forever shy.
While artful artists canvas all they feel,
They show, at least, a picture of their heart;
With little more than words I mark my seal,
Laying silent, showing not their part.
Were making love with you my only aim,
Then surely strength alone would heal my flesh;
But since already love has made me lame
Eternally I'm caught within this mesh.
And what shall be your voice, when once you know?
Will bitter sounds or lovers' tunes you sow?

15

Of thee, my precious one, this is the last.
That fatal love is drunk upon my heart.
The play was set and all the players cast,
Performance done, performers did depart,
The encores linger but within my mind,
'Tis but for me to now make true my tale:
A lovers' myth I'll let my ending find,
My shattered soul will consolation sail;
For you, my love, I'll say you loved me too,
And cherished thoughts forever will ye know,
But now apart, our love we'll not pursue,
And patient minds will always secrets sow.
We'll hurt her not, the one that stands between,
So love will live in silence, never seen.

16

Gentle is the stroke that hits my heart tonight
When I perceive your voice through midnight air;
Divine the sight to touch my eyes that stare
Upon your perfect form carved in night's light.
Simple desires I have: to hold you tight,
And holding so, to know you love and care
As once did Thetis love a man, so rare
A love between a man and goddess bright;
Then know that ours is love so great and true,
A love on which no storm will show its face,
No mountain ever bar, or rather take;
But in this world perfection comes to few,
And so my dream must take its proper place,
In sleep, so I may live my life awake.

17

In cold resolve my tearful feelings freeze,
My brittle eyes make glossy overtures,
But crying ways will not my image please,
Weeping weaknesses draw sodden laws.
By loss of love the tempting floods are called,
Although departure alters not my form,
My beating heart by pain is never fooled,
My tears flow inwards, soothing there the storm
Departing loves within my soul have made.
Withholding sadness in my mortal frame,
And not dispatching gloom where it may fade,
Makes hard the part I play within this game.
But where my show in loveless wonder plays,
My soul does burn alive for passion's ways.

18

I wish these lines in sonnet form were writ,
To tell those time-past tales with finer face;
A shameful mind declares they are not fit,
And shall not live within this story's space.
But Cupid's head is raisèd from his sleep,
For him disturbing passion has no form,
He asks me so these lines of love to keep;
Thus new I'll write, so loss I need not mourn.
I glance upon those lines with lovers' tears,
Deceased is light yet shadows linger still,
Betrayal's dreams are yet amongst my fears,
And cross-eyed love I still would like to kill.
But sweetest memories do stir my mind,
For First-Love's mark upon these lines is signed.

19

Romantic dreams my day-long hours fill,
Perilous my purpose thus is placed,
Misplaced reality will sane souls kill,
But chosen so, my challenge must be faced.
I would my heart and soul were pure for quest,
My innocence were far beyond compare;
Thus armed I'd journey on my mortal test,
Eternal fame they'd grant to deeds I'd dare,
My vital fairytale I long to write,
Long last encounter she who is my life,
The perfect bride of beauteous soul so white;
Though princess she, I'd ne'er make her my wife;
For marriage makes a mix of Fortune's fate,
And perfect love in each night's dreams must wait.

20

Descending walls rise high on either side,
Closing fast around my falling soul,
And grave, I realize now, to be this ride,
Scared screams I hurl as I to darkness roll,
My shout is aimed at thee, "Remembered Dream",
That loss I chose does suffering leave 'til now,
One moment's blow strikes hard about my seam,
And tearing hard does leave me bowing low.
Where play ye now, my soothing, charming sprite?
If e'er in life my fate did cause a need,
Return my love and darkness turn to light,
Lest blackness pierce and suck my soul to feed.
O where upon the path did I thee lose?
Sing lullabies of memories, my muse.

21

When next you rest and to your pillow take,
Be not afraid of what the darkness brings,
And let not dreams your gentle spirit shake,
'Less they be dreams of princes or of kings,
Or dreams of heroes seeking magic rings;
Let Cupid's blissful peace sweep o'er your mind,
Make fast oblivion within his wings,
And then each moon your sleep will solace find
Remember when I sung this song to thee,
When anxious nights did follow troubled days,
And late-night, tear-drained eyes confronted me?
"Fear not" said I to all uneasy ways;
And now I wish those childish troubles back-
I've felt the weight which childish troubles lack.

22

O stranger, you that find this piece of verse.
I hope you come with artful, open mind,
And put not down these lines with childish curse;
If in stale and sour a mood this does you find,
My rhyme, I pray, your day it will make kind,
And if, in love, my words you come to read,
And empty bed you'll not this evening find,
Then leave them here for one in greater need.
If love, Stranger, your way has never looked,
Give leave to me and read upon this scene,
Learn from the muse whose heart is passion cooked:
My look is green where arrows ne'er have been,
But too, for you, my eyes have shed their tears,
For all your life you've faced alone your fears.

23

Hopeful drops of spring-borne rain slide slow
Like shining pearls from Heaven's treasure chest,
Down cheeks, where tears of pain should never flow,
To breasts, where evil hands should never rest.
But seek I not, attention yours, to fetch,
For gloating eyes would mar my valoured form,
So honour bound, one should not ladies leche,
No gentlemen are they who to you swarm.
But will you notice me amongst this crowd?
Nobility must surely pay rewards.
Should princes abdicate and shout out loud,
Amidst that floor of frenzied, drunken lords?
I'll faithful be to she who may be not,
And death I'll see before a lecherous rot.

24

A playful stream my recent verses seem,
Confusion strikes from out this sequence strange,
They flow uneven, lost without a theme,
But need there be a reason for this change?
A scattered mind may often chaos make,
And babbling muses for a sojourn hover;
Disturbing tidings plainly order break,
Dumbfounded ruin strikes to reason bother.
Forgive me thus for jumping tunes so played,
I never meant to break this story's course,
But muses taxing checked my mind so weighed,
Aligned they songs, for better or for worse.
But now the calm appears behind the storm,
And turmoil 's lapsed, forgetting perplexed form.

25

The twilight silence softening my ears,
The summer breeze that warms my lazy heart,
The market roses moving eyes to tears,
And winter snow which falls when Heavens part.
The autumn fall that colours every shade,
The restless waves which break on rocky ground,
And joyous spring, when bitter winds do fade;
These wond'rous roles are by your beauty played.
But weep you not, if this you think you lack,
For beauty's ways are never plain to see;
While golden stars shine out of skies so black,
The perfect soul may not a rosebud be.
For love will never age as age we do,
Not body, but the soul, will make love true.

26

Dispatching melodies of tuneful sorrow
Makes minutes bareful 'til the setting sun,
But testing trials are doubtful battles won,
And soreful loss may come about tomorrow.
My company grows less and less each moon,
Reclusive shyness hides within my eyes,
Retreating fast from people living lies;
Let's place disaster in my diary soon.
The faithful task to which I put myself,
Lays rocky shores apart from present worlds,
Where she within her loving arms me folds,
And there remaining stores my soul to health.
Tear drenched shades shout loud from out my heart,
I know the end is near when nightmares start.

27

Tomorrow's dawn puts forth another watch,
Determined vigil masks a faint despair,
Hypnotic waves do oft perplexion catch,
Submerging troubles washed back to their lair.
With meditation's eye I stand alone,
Rewards for loyalty are problems calmed,
Yet loyalty still brings companions none,
And so my waiting soul remains uncharmed,
A blessing wave will p'haps bring her to shore,
Departing tides may strand her on the sand,
Romantic dreams know nought of nature's law,
I pray I will not disappointed stand.
However life may make a mockery,
Such dreams will see my mermaid swim to me.

28

You never understood the wound you made,
The depth to which you drove the arrow in,
Committing so the dreadful lovers' sin;
My heart bled much to witness your love fade,
So palpable a dream I ne'er did live;
Yet heated moments often stir the mind,
Such moments often will this beauty find,
And, stirring minds will false illusions give.
Why weight is lent towards so fine a form,
Philosophy will not for certain say,
Fair skin must pay among immortal fey,
Yet age will leave us nought to keep us warm.
So, careful be, when you should choose your wife,
For love's true nature shows in later life.

29

What secret message is in memory found?
Why fare the histories of man so well?
Why gather I these sonnet forms to tell?
For whose great destiny will these songs sound?
Will it be he, whose battle tunes are sung?
Inspired by some melodious crusade?
Or tales of romance, lovers' sorrow paid
May be for she, whose thoughts are seaward flung?
Whate'er the fate of dreamers' lines here writ,
They've paid, at least, a little writers' peace;
Problems versed are problems often ceased,
And rhyming memories are ever lit.
So read for pleasure's sake or studious bliss,
This dreamer's tale of verse and memories kiss.

30

The scars of troubled life begin to show;
Review for me, O muse, who placed them there.
'Twas she, for sure, of beauteous skin, so fair
Who struck this heart and caused these lines to flow;
A deadly love, she bent the rules of play,
Wild youthfulness did break the dreamer's wish.
And next there came the mark of soiled flesh,
When love eternal lit the safest way.
But love so true was torn by chestnut eyes,
And bitter struggles pushed to love pursue.
Then came that year of friends both old and new,
When ladies' knights ignored their lovers' cries.
And now there's scratched the biggest scar of all,
This time, when laughter's such a distant call.

31

Did sorrow seek to tell so fine a tale,
Where tragedy did romance lay to rest?
The drama hears the lover's moaning wail
When fate arrives, that uninvited guest.
She's caught me now, the tiding moons are done,
And time is swept beneath this fortune's wave.
Why should I think my struggle would be won,
When ne'er I looked upon the love she gave?
I've lost her now, I barely can believe,
My little one has left, forever gone,
While shattered shafts do strength upon her weave,
And memories of me are memories done.
How could I pass my loved one in the night?
What blindness masks the shine of true-love's light?

32

Do you believe in mermaids swimming free?
Shall I tell thee of most un-fathomed love?
When dreamers seek, enchanted by the sea,
That promised place - no land for tiring doves,
Where ladies glide with soft, seducing strokes,
With reasons none and life's forever young.
There dwells the home of all the mermaid folk
Where soothing lullabies are 'ever sung.
Yet willing thee are you to pay the price?
For love so dear will ne'er be mortal cheap,
The ultimate must be your sacrifice,
Therein the deepest waters must you leap.
Forget these dreams immortal, be not led,
Your true-love waits on land, beside your bed.

33

Broken hearts by loving hands are healed;
Gentle voices, fresh with memory's breath,
Belittle grief when Lovers' lifeblood's spilled,
Once more the hollow heart will finally breathe;
And why deserveth he torments' respite,
He who broke a heart with virgin pain,
With reason none did shadow out her light?
Her first-love's hate caused tears that hid the rain;
Loving so, he looked to love another,
With fast intentions broke compassion's ways;
But fortune saw that failure was his brother,
Accept he must the price he had to pay.
Yet learnt he nought from giving birth to pain!
Past lovers threaten weakness once again.

34

To take my part in festive joy this tide
Would ever be a dream upon this life,
When matching souls would troubled hearts confide,
And lover's words would end this season's strife.
But time has stolen marches more than one,
And late I make the rendezvous again;
Heart pierced and trapped within the web I spun,
My weeping symptoms cry aloud my pain,
And hope is my companion for the while;
Yet fearful stirrings warrant fair display.
I pray to God once more I'll see your smile,
Without your soul the dark brings cold dismay.
So, patiently I'll watch the coast each day,
Lest love's return should stumble by my way.

35

I took my soul away for pleasure's sake,
Perhaps to find a happier way to live,
Yet novelties are quick their leave to take,
And greener grass did little fresh life give;
And once my path had slipped away from sight,
Regret did weave its way around my heart.
Where left I thee when first I took my flight?
I left thee lost with pain to play my part:
"When dreams come true, no longer dreams they be".
Why could I not remember this, with you?
Forgetting so cost me the loser's fee,
And lost is all the love we ever knew.
What foolish knavery did strike my mind?
In whom but you should I my true-love find?

36

Deprived of sleep my body longs to rest,
But minds work fast to bring old memories back;
My tears are sure as sun-down in the west,
And slumber's peace my dreams will surely lack.
Will some soul sing sad songs when I am gone,
As once to love-torn heroes bards did play?
Or will death's icy hand squeeze hard upon
Renown of muses proud, and so betray
The heritage of this love's tragedy?
Light-minded sight should now be my desire,
For lingering love prescribes no remedy;
The shades of time, like ghosts, will ne'er expire.
Yet haunting love induces no regret,
For haunting love resolves I'll ne'er forget.

37

"I love you", once she wrote: "Please love me back";
For want of pleasure's flesh I told her: "no";
With one heart torn in two the pain did wrack
Throughout her spirit fair, a deadly blow.
Now put to trial my conscience pleads its sin:
"Do tell the court why true love you enraged".
In truth I swear I thought not genuine
Th'enamoured manner of our souls engaged.
Defence pathetic could not justice stand,
And: "Lynched by loss is penance adequate".
Reprising further: "friendships are all banned",
And sharpest stones are mine to walk barefoot.
Will sentence never give me my relief?
Or must I write eternal in this grief?

38

How great a task has duty bound to thee?
A lover maid for he who has no love,
A beauteous scene, for he who cannot see,
The first dry land, for he who has no dove.
Which sickly god did burden you with me?
So jovial it is to watch our play!
Act one: I left you, in this tragedy,
Act two: you wished away that fateful day,
And in the third, I walk the stage alone,
The fickle lover finds his love too late;
Be wary of the magic that you've sown,
If once again my love, you contemplate.
Now, Eastern god, a new director cast,
For leading ladies I have lost my last.

39

Why do I hear you speak of other men,
When children are they to my love compared?
When false they'll be, o' time and time again,
And faced by me their valour is too scared?
If one does love you half as much as I
Then to his sword I'll place my bowing head,
But if they cheat and woo you with a lie,
Then passion's strength will feed me 'til they're dead;
Much wasted time 'til all the waiting's done,
Yet waiting doubts you ever will return,
Despite my boasts, I sense another's won;
Eternal more, for restful nights, I'll yearn.
If other eyes should take your passion part,
I'll tear apart my broken lover's heart.

40

What good can come of old wounds struck afresh?
Bemired is now the name I'll mould for thee,
Twice smitten heart cleaved in a lovers' mesh;
Lock now my crypt and hide away the key,
Lest jealous eyes should wreck your union;
Once other lips than mine caress your heart,
I'll ravish darkness at this liaison,
Between our souls will rise a high rampart,
And never more will we love's words exchange.
Confine me quick, devoid me of this sight,
For pity's sake my soul you must estrange,
But, blest be he who next espies your light.
No new love will arrive, my soul, to save,
For wounded twice is truly wounded grave.

41

When sometimes I perceive my mirrored sight,
Reflecting eyes stare strange from silver glass,
The story-tellers of a tearful plight;
I look for tales, in order time to pass.
Should I read fear from out that frightened gaze?
Or is betrayal there the struggle learnt?
And one may see that art of loving ways,
A lesson there within those pupils burnt.
Whose pride has taken looks so young and placed
Therein the wisdom of a lifetime past?
While facing none, all struggles have been faced,
Though loving none, all lovers have been cast.
While beauty does from innocence prevail,
Such tortured learning needs a youthful veil.

42

You wish to learn the tune of women's hearts?
Their loving songs are not unlike your own;
The beating pattern of our counterparts
Is rhythm one with yours once love is sown.
Think not that female grace is injured less
When broken faith doth tip a poisoned shot;
When licking wounds, know that the wounds you dress
Are to her bleeding soul so different not.
Beware your lady lover's tender breast,
Lest she display her vented heart's revenge,
Learn not through trial, this costly knowledge blest,
Play careful pain, and softly hurt avenge.
Forgive me, love, that I considered thee
Immune to anguish, from such torture free.

43

Last night I dreamt of angels in my sleep,
The Heavens whispered in my tired ears,
But slumber held, reward I could not reap,
A senseless waste now feeds my bitter tears.
Forgetting dreams is no mere idle sin,
My laughing love is lost, forever gone,
And echoes ring a painful, crying din;
The fabric of our innocence is torn.
I'll take the pain from verseless love, and write
Upon the wretched reign of misery,
With solitude my bed-mate for the night,
And lay awake each night in disarray.
And if once more those angels should appear,
I'll wake more timely 'pon that dream, my dear.

44

Once more alone, and staring out to sea,
In winter storms my second love has flown,
Though blame must search for no one else but me,
A finer soul than she I've never known;
As questions make my mind to ceaseless work,
I ponder on events that led me here,
The answers in their piteous pits do lurk;
How could my love have grown so insincere?
But, hold upon this chosen course I must,
Decisions made must be decisions played,
And shelved should be our play, to gather dust,
And sep'rate, we will watch the sun-set fade.
Perhaps in days to come we'll browse those shelves,
And find once more some speeches for ourselves.

45

She caught me not by wonder in her eyes,
No magic grace did from her body weave,
Her lovers' net was never snared with lies,
Thus rational thought did ne'er my senses leave,
Unless it were by passing scenes detached;
Such was this lady, 'mong the witches placed,
Who, pure of mind, designs had never hatched,
Whose quenching wine no philtre ever laced.
So thus her heart did grow upon a man,
And truth did beat the rhythm of their song,
As strong as Circe's for the Ithacan;
But, why do foolish heroes wander long?
Once love is true then sail away with she,
Why wave to shore each time you put to sea?

46

Should roses carry thorns upon their stem,
Whilst other flowers wear an easier veil?
Should mountains cover Earth's most precious gem,
When sifting shallow streams will never fail?
Perhaps a sign, for those who roses mind,
That beauteous form will often danger shape?
Or warning dire, for those who diamonds find,
That trembling caves may threaten their escape?
Yet know a meaning more than omens few,
And reason that the pain in love's desire
Contrives assurance for the suitor true:
The purest tune will need the dearest lyre.
Should roses carry thorns upon their stem?
For truest love my soul I would condemn.

47

Hush, listen to the cries of children lost:
Their piteous wails are barely audible,
The warmest hands will be as winter's frost,
And rotten foods will scarce be edible.
A little boy, alone upon a hill,
No mother calls his name with anxious might,
No memories of home to heat his will,
No sadness could portray the exile's flight.
But wrong am I to match these fates to mine:
Where homes are lost I have my warm abode,
Where souls have died I hear no suff'ring whine,
Where future's spent I have at least this road.
But still, my fate, will cruelest of them be,
For tragedy of choice was lent to me.

48

"She loves you very much" in converse spoke,
Some warming words that soothed my battered soul,
For here was love that never would me choke,
And never would it play a vengeful role,
For love 'twixt friends is rare enough to find,
Since here, this love knows not of Cupid's bow,
No potioned arrow will, the senses, blind,
And Puck has not his devious tricks to sow;
Your shoulders damp are cradles for a child,
Embracing arms are shrouds to keep me warm,
Not kissing mantles for a passion wild,
Or envious trials when others to them swarm.
So knowing thee I'm glad I troubles feel,
My soul is still when I beside thee kneel.

49

Inspired by driving want to watch the waves,
I stood today above a churning din,
Onlookers downwards gloat, and say: "He saves
His tale of love for Nature's ears to win".
'Tis more than love I give the raging sea;
I lend the produce of my careful thought,
And muses' words the blue returns to me,
Inspired in the deep, by mermen wrought.
We're almost at the last; I feel the age
Of youth-torn love departing from these lines,
And great the pain of ages gone does gauge
Its height by tears and broken, crying signs.
O live again this time of summers past,
Rise once more sun, you have not shone your last.

50

This is a fitting place to write this song;
Love's end should meet the place where love began,
The battle now should turn to right and wrong,
Philosophy should set a verse for man.
The poet's done and matched his love with words,
No 'middle bitch' will write to rival this,
No reddened verse will need replace my swords;
A muse upon my shoulder did me kiss.
But, how is worth put to a measure made?
If life has never knocked your heart you're dead;
So touched am I that love has with me laid,
For she was wise and well my senses fed.
And how should I make now this couplet theme?
I thank thee most, my sweet Remembered Dream.

III

Sonnets of Philosophy

1 On Philosophy

A note to touch the chords of those who've played,
A word to open eyes that never read,
A warmth to chase the chill when summers fade,
A hand to hold the wounds of those who bleed;
These lines do mark the realm of thinking men
Where questions lie on every path of life,
And answers lay beyond the writer's pen;
Solutions sought so often cause a strife,
When conflict puts to war confusing minds,
With answers dealt like cats which chase their tails,
A backward leap - the product of these finds,
No comfort sole to tread this path of nails.
'Sophia hear!' - for answers I'm too weak,
'Tis but the questions I'll attempt to seek.

2 On Self-Doubt

What judge am I to harvest better crop?
To lift the veils of brides for future men?
No virgin's tears my naked fingers stop,
And oft my words are writ with reddened pen.
While taint and shame plays with our mortal souls,
Learn depth from this, our sin original;
By questions gleam an answer to your role,
And lay a path of life more bountiful.
Thus doubting man will yield the finest fruit,
Promoting change, and doubting patterns known,
So, doubt the flat, and round will surely suit,
And making sure to doubt the doubt that's grown.
But harvest little from this preaching tale,
For preachers' words do oft their preachers fail.

3 On Truth

A search for truth is but a venture flawed,
Miscast is reason played upon this quest,
Like poorest actors seeking fine applaud,
Truth finding venturers will find no rest.
But not because the treasure sought is false,
For truth is palpable, to vision clear
And beats a path through life with monstrous pulse,
But searching far bows low to searching near,
For truth is hidden by simplicity.
So mark each pace with truth on every heel,
'Tis there to choose in each man's destiny,
The least may wield the truth as humble steel,
For what are we if this we do not know?
This purest god, as white as winter snow.

4 On Choice

Damned human souls leave footprints in the snow,
A sharp reminder of our mortal weight,
But, see the stamping made by some who go
With conscience none to prick the ears of fate.
The human drive is led by history's sin,
And human souls are by dilemma faced,
A bastard choice, yet leaving chance to win
A seat divine, a seat in heaven placed.
For God gives us a chance to choices see,
That he may love our heavy-burdened souls,
And, what is God with no forbidden tree?
The thoughtless father of a man not whole.
For what are we if choice we do not make?
A foolish clown whose painted life is fake.

5 On The Warrior

Count well our children falling to the sword,
Despairing pleas are masked by bloody rage;
Whose faithful men are these and by whose word
Do battle-lords, this conflict sour, engage?
No honoured tongue shall call them warriors,
Naivety shines through their gory shields,
Plain, mindless soldiers are these conquerors,
Though heroed shrines might litter all their fields.
True fighting men need never take up sword,
Since stand they always must for what is right,
And weapons oft will be a simple word,
Such mighty struggles need true warriors' might,
For what are we when we give way to rage?
So careful must we be to war engage.

6 On Loneliness

The price of loneliness seems fair to me,
Inspired invention torn from privacy
Keeps proud the slant of my philosophy,
Considered thought is shy in company,
Or so my soul secluded found it so;
The bitter cost was frozen on my mind,
But life was warmed beneath this fur of snow,
And reason bloomed a flower as crowds declined;
Shall now these lessons learnt be sure enough?
When will this lonely war-lord come to rest?
Though much is known the path is growing rough,
Will fortune send to me a saving guest?
For now I have a clearer need in life:
A soul who's heard this silence as my wife.

7 On Beauty

If certain looks are by the angels made,
Then does some fiendish sprite the others cast?
How fine a touch the heav'nly spirits laid
Upon the charming face by beauty masked;
Yet harpies gross do grow a stunning half,
A siren lure to catch a flound'ring man,
As beauteous song gives way to demon's laugh
The haunted soul will see where form began.
A grace-like face is nature's gift to give,
Whilst heart and soul, a mortal's game to play,
And so we must with God and nature live,
Make honest love, and find our heaven's way.
For certain looks are by the angels made,
Yet certain looks by truth are seldom weighed.

8 On Madness

No keener sense to find the words I need,
This insane hold leaves prints of talents new,
Creative force from un-sound throats does bleed,
A prophet's words to huddled masses woo;
A pressured mind may spew out endless thought,
Haephaestus born, the senses will explode,
By heavy ashes swarming crowds are caught,
Whilst few will find the diamond codes there sowed.
So, how doth stand this wisdom in the rough?
And who shall sift the filth and sort the good?
A prophet born to sort the puzzle tough!
With profit none the crowd is empty stood.
But madness needs a madman sound of mind,
For pseudo-sane will pseudo-favour find.

9 On purity

Illiterate men would read this poem best,
A blinded man would see the lines most well,
Whilst deaf the man to hear above the rest,
And dumb the soul to others these lines tell.
For purity is not a man-made sound,
Its words will fail to form by mortal pen,
No shape or mould will by our eyes be found,
The ears that hear her sound are not of men.
Once evil reason breeds her power to will,
A purity divine is inhumane,
For life must harvest sin, and pure ways kill,
The power to live may pure souls only feign.
So, if a spirit pure you chance upon,
Dismiss her smart, before you do her wrong.

10 On Religion

While safe inside religion's fort you preach,
A million souls search hard for what you've lost.
For solid ends and sure reward you teach,
While we who follow God know well his cost,
In snared belief you buy your passage firm,
And God will love you less for passage smooth;
Yet come and spend with me in church a term,
I'll show you troubled choice of holy truth.
A million gods will send their prophets wise,
Yet shelter not in any words of theirs,
Choose well your ground, and stand against the lies,
Buy none of all the prophet-mongers' wares.
I need no word from God to love him well,
Bind not yourself in man's religious cell.

11 On Love

Whose melted passion burns from out these eyes?
How like your sight to signal love ignite!
Beware, the soul may weave a dread disguise,
I've felt the victim pain of blinkered sight;
Yet still my eyes wax wide with love's design,
When painful forms of female grace I spy,
So real, my fated match must be this fine,
A love with mirage less would be a lie,
In romance tales the princess must be fair,
And frog turns so to prince and duck to swan,
Did any dream a tale with plainer pair?
And so my heart will beauty gaze upon.
Perhaps I wish that I was born sight blind,
Then sightless, love my soul would better find.

12 On Shyness

For tragedy my character is set,
Those senses, once again, prove paranoid,
And others' words are with harsh judgement met,
So scared to burn, I'll others' sight avoid;
With creatures of the night I hide my face,
To walk upon the darkened shore I choose,
With lustful markets none, just empty space;
Though lonely now my search, I will not lose,
For lonely souls will lonely hearts attract,
And love is blind, 'less love is heart attached;
While previous love my body may have lacked,
By knightly quest my love is heaven matched.
While shyness, though, might blight a youthful heart,
No compromise will steal my tragic part.

13 On Innocence

My sonnet lines are now for sadness set,
A chol'ric mode to sound the bitter years,
Where great annoyance weaves a fine-spun net,
And disappointment swells the dam of tears;
What bastard yields have grown from out this world?
So foul a crop is from foul nurture sown,
Disjointed gods have paradise unfurled,
And torn their tythe 'til fields are barren stone.
Wake up to life, o child of innocence,
But know most well that innocence is learnt,
A compliment born not from ignorance,
But, said of those whose souls were never burnt.
The purest soul must earn such just station,
Innocence needs most its temptation.

14 On War

I know not why those men go marching by,
Though skin and words do match the tone of mine,
It grieves me so to watch these women cry,
Though know I not their reason most malign.
A far-off call to speed to warring lands,
And as I plot my reasons why to war,
I hear the drums of eager, vengeful bands,
This carnage want does foul God's natural law;
Break not my heart with soldiers' fighting sounds,
Be slow to draw, and know your target well,
These fields are full of crossed, unanswered mounds,
Forgotten souls, alone in darkness, fell.
Be careful then your uniform to choose,
That life should die, your conscience you'll not lose.

15 On Courage

What courage this, from those who have no choice?
No single option needs false flattery,
If fate demands then sing no praising voice,
Make full applause where you dilemma see.
A coward man may watch a sailor drown,
We are obliged when we the drowning hear,
Poor choice it is to wear the coward's crown,
Courageous men should know too well their fear;
And you, brave soldier, on the bloody field,
You follow well your orders to obey,
With courage none so many have you killed
Who chose to stand and die upon this day.
My sword is sharp and ready quick to kill,
But choice I need my courage part to fill.

16 On Wealth

One night I dreamt a figure in my sleep,
A slender waist and struggled gait I saw,
A dying child did down beside him creep,
No tears were left inside those eyes so raw,
A helping hand I held towards his face,
And welcome was the grasp he took of this,
For, at his touch I saw the worser case:
Deformed, my belly did the dry earth kiss,
And struggled he to lift me from the ground;
My gaping eyes, so used to waste perverse
Had now the basic needs of life just found,
Damned idle minds, afford creative curse.
'Choose well', he spoke, 'Your life is hard to stand',
'Your camel rides the needles, mine - just sand'.

17 On Honesty

Most touching words are of one's honesty,
A finer quality you need not seek,
And always truth should be your policy,
A future warped with lies is future bleak.
So basic are the rules of honest play,
No weaving needles spun to draw our blood,
No sympathy malign to bar our way,
No creeping harm grown from a lying bud.
With honest truth strike well your killing blow,
With honest plan lay sound philosophy,
With true approach, firm is the path you go,
Test not your lies against divinity:
If conscience false does sound a scheming way,
Weave well your lies to wear on judgement day.

18 On Romance

A coupled walk across a moonlit bay,
A listening ear to hear the names of stars,
A soothing touch, a soul on which to lay,
Fine company, to count away the hours.
Is this the dream of those romantic souls?
Those lonely souls who search eternally?
I hope they know the truth behind their roles,
For never will they find their courtship key.
Since, 'romance-true' is tragic, start to end,
For coupled love brings harsh reality,
Romantic dreams may not existence tend,
For 'true-love' has no place in tragedy.
So wander long you brave, romantic fool,
Your quest must fail, or false would be your call.

19 On God

Who does not love the mischief in their hearts?
I've sung of lures that prove the purest soul,
And is there man where bait has played no part?
No child of God avoids temptation's role;
And what of bliss, before that fruit was wrest?
Such lonely bliss, to need creation fresh,
And what of God, did He need such a test?
A need to love did shape the devil's flesh.
Forsake me then and learn the love I give,
Make sad my fate and learn my happiness,
Then take my life and learn the joy to live,
Make failure mine and learn of my success.
I love You so, yet hate You when You fail,
Though power whole, You'll ne'er be human frail.

20 On Happiness

How happy are the thieves of others' loss?
How satisfied the hangman cutting-down?
How feels revenge with foes upon the cross?
How glorified the king with bloody crown?
What piece of happiness is then your aim?
Should we accept the scholars of the past?
Happy, they said, was he who found no blame,
The happiest man may be a down outcast,
A man who strives to do the world no harm,
And lay about the rest his wisdom true,
Thus Croesus learned, and gave Cyrus alarm,
O wretched Socrates, we are so few.
And thus I wish when joy and I do flirt
That conscience mine knows none my laughter hurts.

21 On Sympathy

When water to my thirsty tree I give,
I save her life, but so with consequence,
For p'haps this tree no longer was to live,
And now this fate has changed nature's events;
The beasts of field do oft their offspring kill,
And so, should I put them within my care
And thus exert upon their lives my will?
Before I came, how well did nature fare?
But, science now has found this lucky earth!
An action made will show reaction played,
A wisdom true since woman knew of birth,
O newborn man this earth will never fade!
This sympathy you've found is meant for you,
An honest rule to guide your conscience new.

22 On The Poet

A tragic verse brings joy to many hearts,
Enlightened poets toil with words of grief,
Delighting muses of the tragic arts,
And muses cruel will never lend relief,
Lest happiness should lend their poets rest,
And drawn are they who cannot write these songs,
To match their words, and run the tragic test,
Inspired by nought to lay in verse life's wrongs,
These tuneless amateurs are verse's curse,
The truth of poets lies within their work,
The sweet-lyred muse does tortured life emburse,
Inspiring tunes where tortured life does lurk.
The verse that lies un-touched by pain divine,
Is verse not fed upon the muse's wine.

23 On Memory

'You should not live within your memory,
Your private thoughts should match the present need'.
Advice in vain the hypocrite lent me,
For desperate loss had stirred good memory's seed.
Memories, like seasons, go their round,
Your diary mind, a souvenir unique -
Upon its shelves are tales of nature found,
Of spring-born youth and endless winter bleak,
Past summers' harvest bring you peace of mind,
And autumn's thoughts are food to feed your soul;
So rest upon these relics foul and kind,
The future's plans must lessons past enrol.
Look well within this theatre of your mind,
A season sweet you should in memories find.

24 On Summer

What lessons, then, can we from summer learn?
Exciting season, warm with laziness,
When passion's fire does tender bodies burn,
And heated hearts plunge into craziness;
Next-door's children shout aloud their years,
Whilst pretty girls pass laughing, beachward bound,
And summer's romance casts away all fears
As summer's waves break to a peaceful sound;
With easy love and easy smiles abroad,
The westward breeze does bring its seasoned charm,
Whilst farmers toil, new lovers sneak toward
Enchanted woods to summer's customs farm.
This season's taste is hot with passions strong,
Come autumn soon lest they be passions wrong.

25 On Autumn

Equator lands burn lessons harsh on life,
While autumn freshness chills our summer love,
The tree-sprite trims each branch with autumn's knife,
As varied hues are cast by autumn's glove.
A lonely time, as summer friends depart,
Emotion charged, as nature battles death,
Reflective times, before the snows do start,
Creation contrasts well in autumn's breath,
For tragic are the shades of autumn hue,
And tragedy does drive creative bliss;
Weep not that summer nights are but too few,
Meet well this loss, respond to autumn's kiss.
This season cool, a twilight simile,
So near to death, yet free from misery.

26 On Winter

The summer-winter season now has gone,
Extreme must be the passion from here on,
And strong must be the shelter's foundation,
For winter storms have come with mercy none.
The season-king for misery adverse,
A clutch of tempests held in either hand,
Commanding winter marks his power perverse,
His icy hands guide terror to our land.
And more than death, he spawns an after-life,
Where monsters born from out mythology
Ride far and wide on fearful storms of strife -
A turmoil foul, to fill chronology.
This season tastes of lovers wrapped as one,
Whilst poets freeze, their bodies wrapped with none.

27 On Spring

Could it be true that summer's sun I see?
And can I hear the laughter in the air?
Could winter's storms have raised their last on me?
Has spring arrived with all its weather fair?
And now that joy has threatened here to bloom,
I sense a loss as snow-flakes turn to rain,
For memories dear had shared my empty room,
The north-flung gales did compliment my pain;
In spring arrives the planting with first sun,
As April rains prepare the fertile ground,
So fresh this feeling - new life just begun,
Twice blest are they who new love here have found.
Creation ripe does not the muse caress,
For spring gives rise to blandest happiness.

28 On Suffering

I knew a boy who suffered for a while,
And even now, though gone those sorry days,
I sense discomfort deep within his smile,
In certain lights his eyes betray their glaze;
Look any time, with friends he's never seen,
Yet, watch the sun retire unto the sea,
You'll catch him there, amid that show serene,
His hidden thoughts can't mask his misery.
'Tis nature's part to make us suffer so,
For few may watch the sunrise pure of heart,
And of these pains, so rare are those who know
The lessons precious, born of sorrow's part.
Humility within us all is found,
Don't carve her out, but build upon her ground.

29 On The Humble

My songs compare like childrens' to a god,
Towards the Great Ones look for wisdom's touch,
Their thoughts are sense against my mutt'rings odd,
Their shoulders' muse does greater knowledge clutch;
Yet false I'd be to call off my attack,
My humble pride must not be checked by fire,
Though rank and file my words should not turn back,
My task divine must be to hold this lyre.
The German writes of false humility,
A cowards' band, far from the field of war,
Where humble claim does safety guarantee,
And from their ranks no thinking men you'd draw.
So I shall lay upon the line my verse,
Then I, at least, will earn my humble curse.

30 On Standards

What use are standards when we let them fall?
Superfluous guidance, wasted in decay;
Compassion false demands respect for all,
Whilst progress is the victim of this play.
Upon the battle-field surrender not,
Or quick will be the stroke that cuts you down,
Pretence deludes the soul and starts the rot,
Dishonest deeds will only evil crown.
Judge harsh your tasks and test your role in life,
A standard less your weakness will exploit,
When failings sour deploy amid some strife,
Perverse, that line rewards the maladroit.
Ambition check and patience gold employ,
Give each your best and glory false destroy.

31 On Change

Black shadows are the ghosts of memories past,
They haunt my creeping soul with happy lure,
To linger long would doubt on futures cast,
A time when change may be the only cure.
Don't hesitate to play the game ahead,
Your suitors true must face the challenge new,
Or suitor true will never share your bed -
Forever lost may be your destined cue.
Once character is bound within your mould,
Accept the offer of your daily quest,
For heroes strong are found within your fold,
And only are they proved by charming quest.
This change must be the trial upon our time,
Variety must tempt our part divine.

32 On Adventure

Adventure must its head seductive rise,
And with it all the fear of Peril's beast,
For, from the darkness hear my boredom cries,
So let me on the light of danger feast.
What bounds are laid upon the laws of life?
Is nature's fear not good to be my friend?
Why shall I not take risk to be my wife?
With menace none I'll not my wisdom blend.
Yet so Achilles spoke until he died,
That deadly shot which took his life, it's said,
Took worthless glory and adventurous pride,
Yet none will learn, until they too are dead.
Take heed of all your mother's loving pleas,
You break her heart when jeopardy you tease.

33 On The Dark

I wonder not why children fear the dark,
It's there to hide what we should never see,
On all our souls the dark has left its mark,
In night-time's darkest dreams there'll blackness be.
And should we teach our youth to darkness tread?
From which to conquer our unwatching foes?
Or would this treachery, with ally dread
Be like to fouling nature's precious rose?
For darkness is a chain that binds us all,
A woven net which we are blind to sense,
A net to cast for no-one save a fool,
A black-hour trap of knavery intense.
So much is pleasant in the life we live,
Yet much is sour when we to darkness give.

34 On Death

I'll write no songs to ease your worried mind,
The nameless state of death will touch us all,
Apologies you'll not in these lines find,
And silence cold will answer when you call.
If death you think will never come to you,
But life anew will let death pass you by
And mortal fears for you do not stand true -
I'll tell you cold: this life you lead's a lie.
If absent are the pains of evil tides,
Then why not absent too your happiness?
The joyful times that often life provides
Are double fold to those who death address.
Prepare each thought as though it is your last,
Lest fate should choose this day to break death's fast.

35 On Fear

I'd hide beneath my bed sheets for the night,
Though soon I'd suffocate for lack of air,
Yet, hidden so would heal me of my fright,
And lying low would lessen so the scare;
Though darkness lingers under covers warm,
And little shield would make this sleeping sheet,
A thousand children to this shelter swarm
When agile minds do with the darkness meet.
Though little safety does this place afford,
Within our mind, a fortress strong we keep,
And monsters out must with our mind accord
And fly away when we to covers creep.
Thus see our fears by childish tricks destroyed,
In minds alone are fear and calm deployed.

36 On Abuse

I'll tear the hearts from those who justice wreck,
And so commit my soul to murderous trial;
Adoring folk of wealth I'll conscience check,
Lest they exploit our home with evil smile;
Night and day must share this natural world,
For each alone would cause un-natural strife,
This foul abuse would see a hell unfurled,
For balanced power must be the force of life.
Take heed when tempting lures you may employ,
Improper use does not your sane soul grip
And dark attachments don't your form destroy,
For balance none could cause a fatal trip.
Accept with strength the fortunes of your fate,
Lest your abuse should raise my passion's hate.

37 On Hate

I've come apart through foul and bloody rage,
Will nothing stop this hate from growing strong?
My reddened soul will taint the poet's page,
And blood must feed my thirst for summers long;
A lover's touch could kill this spell of hate,
And break the season of my loveless track,
Or will the lover's hand bring tears irate?
Forgotten are the teeth of this attack.
And all I know is hate will eat me whole,
No scattered piece of soul will lay in rest,
No chance for love to play it's gentle role,
No time to find in life the life that's best.
Now hatred is a part I've played so well,
Ingrained so hard, I'll not this part dispel.

38 On Friendship

For many souls I knew I'd risk my life,
Yet few would draw my tears if death they met,
And many hearts command my fighting knife,
Yet faces few into my heart I'd let.
What power most in friendship do I feel?
The laughter in the air when friends do speak?
Their mirrored tears when I my problems tell?
Or maybe warmth upon an outlook bleak?
So many friends are but a name to me,
And rare are names that answer when I call,
And true must be the shout to friendship plead,
For with your tears so too your friend will fall.
And, as you count the hearts who'll ease your role,
Mark well the ones who truly know your soul.

39 On Inspiration

From where will come the words of muses lost?
So fast can little changes alter thoughts,
A tragic state demands so foul a cost,
And other moods may not with muses sport.
Why change must come I cannot answer well,
For all good things were pains that did inspire,
And painless life leaves no sad tale to tell,
The comic stands and poets would retire.
Yet, though your words are closed in pages old,
And dull is now the gleam of swords at rest,
Make sure each winter moon when nights are cold,
Your soul remembers hard your tragic test.
The saddest tales sound golden melody,
And where are you without your tragedy?

40 On Women

No rhyming words I'd dare to put for Eve,
Creating here a general slant of mind
Would vast and fatal traps for certain weave
And far afield you would the pieces find.
For praising so the fairest bodies soft,
I would insult the ladies of the sword;
And siding strong with manners high aloft,
Those virtues scarlet then would be ignored.
And so this song should be a comic verse,
For never will I offer words straight faced,
When coins of many shapes make up the purse:
To save their skin the wise write laughter laced.
Yet such is certain of these creatures fair,
The truest one of all shall be my prayer.

41 On Deception

And who shall judge the mouth that lies to thee,
And pain the heart that leads your soul astray?
Deception grew like fruit upon the tree,
And, tasted once, grows fresh inside each day.
So shattered is a heart by love deceived,
And broken is a mind by faith betrayed;
I thought that love was free from fraud conceived,
I thought that faith with honest truth was made.
Yet love and faith have broken both my heart,
And foolish words and deeds I too employed,
Though, at the time, I missed their falsehood part,
Through mutual guile we now are both destroyed.
Yet, one man's truth is sure another's lie,
No envied task of judgement once we die.

42 On Time

At what age will I feel the pinch of time?
When pretty looks no longer my way stare?
Or, when my written words are hard to rhyme?
Yet, beauteous words and looks were always rare . . .
So, can this youthful veil be past its age?
Or is the trial of time yet to begin?
Is now this wisdom set to match the sage?
My childish folly boasts my greatest sin.
Again! What age I'll feel my pinch of time?
Whose wizened face would best my question take?
Is old respite from love for me a crime?
What charming pain do youthful lovers make?
Be still, I say, enjoy your living years,
Let not the pain of youth bring forth these tears.

43 On Pain

What sound does pain make when she tears your heart?
What guise arrays her when she takes the field?
What touch will hers be when she makes you start?
What stench has she breathed over those she's killed?
No room to market all her deadly skills,
No depth can gauge the chasm of her trials,
And none, once born, may flee those mortal ills,
And anguish now may be your yester smiles,
For who can know the conscience of a friend?
No link will serve to know another's mind,
No more than trust may you your lover lend,
So often will you broken lovers find.
Lay well your faith that you might pain avoid,
Make good your love, lest you may be destroyed.

44 On Sleep

The poet now as old as time itself,
A heavy contrast to his early years,
A dusty book now rests upon the shelf,
Long gone are all the streams of youthful tears.
Who would have known that after all that pain,
When night had crept upon the spirits grave,
That Love might wake the happy soul again,
And restless nights might strike this Cupid's slave?
We looked and saw the anguish in your heart;
We heard the sleeping notes that marked your rest;
The moon shone strong and played its soothing part,
No thoughts of dawn could from your dreams you wrest.
Since in your sleep your memories you hold dear,
But wake, dear soul, the future you must fear.

45 On the Contest

Tonight my heart will bleed until I sleep,
The moon will cast her form within my tears,
So, when she rises next I will not weep,
When you will come to bring alive my fears;
Before your eyes my crying will be done,
No broken heart of mine should upset you,
The memories you'll keep will be of fun,
My love for you will not your soul pursue;
And this, I pray, will be my strategy,
And may your words strike quick and to the heart,
And put me not in Lovers' malady,
When you will tell me that our love must part.
And now I'll cry, until my mind is blurred,
Since I am not the love whom you preferred.

46 On the Sunset

You've never seen the sun set in the sea,
You've never strolled across a moonlit beach,
And both these things I want to give to thee,
And giving so, my love for thee I'll teach.
And have you ever loved beneath the stars,
With God and all the saints to bless your act?
For all of heaven's love will then be ours,
When once we kiss and seal our lover's pact.
Could any other touch compare with mine?
Is any other kiss so passion filled,
When I caress your fragile form divine,
Or mark our love when lovers' lips are sealed?
But, how shall we now play the part we've made?
Will it with shattered hearts or love be paid?

47 On Heartache

And what will be my words when you must leave,
When you decide our love has now expired?
Will I, some cunning speech, think fast and weave,
Or, for your sake, say too my love has tired?
And will the fight be done unto its end?
Or, will your judgement foul and leave too soon?
And, if I went away what would I send?
Each day I'd send a rose and lover's tune.
But, when you hold my hand, where are your thoughts?
Are they with me or on your future laid?
For ours is such a fragile love of sorts,
So, every night I pray it may not fade.
But, though you're here, I can't believe it's true,
My fear is that our moments more are few . . .

48 On the Rose

What colour grows the rose I'll give to thee?
I fear it may reflect a painful white,
To mark the close of love for you and me,
And put an end to this, my painful fight.
Or might it bloom and cast a lover's red?
I pray the dawn may in its shade be shown,
And you and I shall make our lovers' bed,
And, there within, a romance will be grown.
I promised you my death if your heart broke,
I was the first to cry because of you,
And when I let you go, my heart did choke,
To show my love for you was cut so true.
What colour grows the rose I'll give to thee?
I fear you may be blind to colour see.

49 On The Meeting

What lies my mind has laid upon my heart
Which, beating blind, has beaten out of time,
Thrice broken now by lovers set to part,
My words of darkness now are sure to rhyme.
I thought that when you came these lines would end,
And you would be the light within my soul,
And lovers' songs these thoughts my heart did lend,
In love, my life did once again seem whole.
But, now my heart puts questions to this mind:
"If love is ours then why is she not here?"
"Why can I, Mind, find tears upon our face?"
Another broken heart, my deepest fear.
And when you say that we must meet to talk,
Why do I sense your tongue will show a fork?

50 On the Adventure

Whose odyssey could match the Ithacans?
So humble are the tales we write today,
A bland conformity posts guardians,
And tests the wills of heroes here to stay.
In all our souls there lay adventures vast,
Yet few select will chance their part to play,
And many virtuous men will ne'er be cast,
Reward they'll miss until their judgement day.
Yet, hear this tale I put for thee in verse,
Where else will be the learning for our young?
A tale of life so rich and bitter curse,
A tale of wisdom, by the muses sung.
For every hero kin to Henry Mask,
A thousand die with none to sing their task.